Happy Birthday To
my "in house expert" on
Vitruvian Architecture! with love
as said before, to Another!
from one goddess Dianne
July 8, 2004

Victorian Cottage Architecture
An American Catalog of Designs, 1891

George F. Barber

INTRODUCTION BY

Michael A. Tomlan

Associate Professor and Director
Graduate Program in Historic Preservation Planning
Cornell University

DOVER PUBLICATIONS, INC.
Mineola, New York

Bibliographical Note

This Dover edition, first published in 2004, is an unabridged republication of *The Cottage Souvenir No. 2: Containing One Hundred and Twenty Original Designs in Cottage and Detail Architecture*, originally published by S. B. Newman & Co., Knoxville, TN, 1891. The introduction by Michael A. Tomlan entitled "Toward the Growth of an Artistic Taste" and which has been included in this edition, is from the 1982 reprint of *The Cottage Souvenir No. 2* originally published by the American Life Foundation and Study Institute, Watkins Glen, New York.

Library of Congress Cataloging-in-Publication Data

Barber, George F. (George Franklin), 1854–1915.
    [Cottage souvenir no. 2]
    Victorian cottage architecture : an American catalog of designs, 1891 / George F. Barber ; introduction by Michael A. Tomlan.—dover ed.
      p. cm.
    Originally published: The cottage souvenir no. 2. Knoxville, Tenn.: S.B. Newman & Co., printers, 1891. With new introd.
    Introd. is from the 1982 reprint of "The Cottage souvenir, no. 2," originally published by the American Life Foundation and Study Institute, Watkins Glen, N.Y.
    Includes bibliographical references and index.
    ISBN 0-486-42990-3 (pbk.)
    1. Architecture, Victorian—United States—Designs and plans. 2. Architecture, Domestic—United States—Designs and plans. I. Title.

NA7207.B37 2004
728'.37'097309034—dc22

                                       2003067488

Manufactured in the United States of America
Dover Publications, Inc., 31 East 2nd Street, Mineola, N.Y. 11501

Toward the Growth of an Artistic Taste

by

Michael A. Tomlan

iv

FIGURE 1   A Sales Tag, c. 1878

Toward the Growth of an
ARTISTIC TASTE

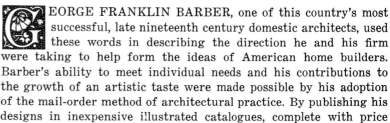

All over America, the idea is spreading that a new building must be original, not thereby meaning a freakish departure from well known principles of design, but one planned originally for the owner. This is right, and will do more toward the growth of an artistic taste and the establishment of content in the homes of the people than any factor which can be employed . . . .[1]

GEORGE FRANKLIN BARBER, one of this country's most successful, late nineteenth century domestic architects, used these words in describing the direction he and his firm were taking to help form the ideas of American home builders. Barber's ability to meet individual needs and his contributions to the growth of an artistic taste were made possible by his adoption of the mail-order method of architectural practice. By publishing his designs in inexpensive illustrated catalogues, complete with price lists for his drawings (and even with order forms), Barber reached thousands of potential clients throughout the United States and abroad. Recently, as Americans have once again begun to accept and even to embrace the artistic taste of which Barber was speaking, dozens of his "original" designs have been rediscovered. Within the past decade, "Barber Houses"[2] have been repeatedly cited as "unique," "fascinating," and "distinctive." A number of them have been photographed for periodicals, books, and state or local architectural inventories. Many have been "restored" (at least three of which have become house museums), others have been sketched and printed for Christmas cards and wall hangings, and one design has even been built in miniature and sold as a doll house. *The Cottage Souvenir No. 2* which follows in facsimile provides us not only with a record of Barber's first attempt to reach a national market, but also with the opportunity to study as a collection some of his most popular designs.

Although George Franklin Barber was born in July 1854, in De Kalb, Illinois, he grew up on a farm near Marmaton, Kansas, just eight miles west of Fort Scott, with the family of his older sister, Olive, and her husband, William Barrett.[3] His only formal education was sporadic, punctuated by local unrest and the Civil War. He took an early, active interest in rock collecting and horticulture, and on at least one occasion sent an entire collection of wood and rock specimens to his older brother, Manley DeWitt Barber, in De Kalb.[4] The interest in horticulture seems to have become a part-time commitment by early manhood, for in 1878 he signed a deed making him the sole owner of a farm adjacent to that of the Barrett family,[5] and a sales tag has survived indicating that he was a dealer in "Ornamental Nursery Stock." At the same time, however, Barber's occupation on tax assessment receipts is listed as a "carpenter."[6]

FRONTISPIECE   George F. Barber (1854–1915)

The question of precisely when Barber first became actively interested in the construction of buildings can be answered only indirectly. There is a legend in the Barber family that he displayed an early interest in artistic matters; recollections of one person picture him drawing in the mud with a stick, while other children were more actively occupied.[7] The first evidence of his interest in architecture *per se* is a notebook entitled "Civil Architecture, 1873," in which Barber sketched several pages of architectural elements and wrote a short description of each. The variety of Classical and Gothic details, and the various elementary geometrical exercises included in the notebook suggest that Barber educated himself by copying a dictionary-like handbook.

While the extent and nature of his architectural library at this time is not known, some of Barber's acquisitions in the ensuing years can be documented. In 1876, for example, Barber made a number of purchases from the booksellers and publishers A. J. Bicknell & Co. of New York. Among these were several volumes in "Weale's Rudimentary Series"—English handbooks noted for their technical information, including those on mechanics, acoustics, building, and architectural modelling. Another book, *Palliser's American Cottage Homes*, was inscribed "G. F. Barber, Fort Scott, Kansas, February 7, 1883;" this would have been available through Bicknell's successor, William T. Comstock.[8] Other publications, including periodicals, may well have been purchased but not survived because they were bound as paperbacks or were merely unbound newsprint. Thus it becomes clear that Barber's architectural education, as well as his method of practice, was largely dependent upon the U. S. Mail.

Although Fort Scott was experiencing a building boom as a major railroad junction for southeast Kansas, Barber left by 1884 to rejoin the majority of his relatives in De Kalb.[9] This move may have been in response to an opportunity to assist his older brother, Manley DeWitt Barber, a respected house carpenter in the area. At this time George's training and concern for the everyday problems of the carpenter resulted in the patent specifications for his "Nail Holding Attachment for Hammers."

The attachment will be found very useful for carpenters and others on high buildings as the operator may hold himself securely with one hand while doing the nailing with the other, thus avoiding the necessity of a scaffold or the placing of a ladder for driving a few nails . . . ." [10]

While there is no record of whether or not this simple spring clip was ever produced, even today most carpenters would see the merit of Barber's invention.

As was indicated by the books he had purchased, however, Barber thought of building not simply as a carpenter, but as a designer. By the mid-1880s he was acting as architect for the firm of Barber and Boardman, Contractors and Builders, apparently involved with many residential structures.[11] Undoubtedly the largest known building of his early career was the Congregational Church, which still stands at the corner of Grove and Second Streets in De Kalb. A rather detailed account of the construction of the church, written by Manley DeWitt Barber and published in a local newspaper, noted it was begun in late September 1885, and finally completed in mid-1888.[12]

While enjoying considerable success, Barber's often poor health made it necessary for him to leave De Kalb for the more salubrious climate found in the mountains of East Tennessee. Arriving in Knoxville in late 1888 with his wife and newborn child, Barber set

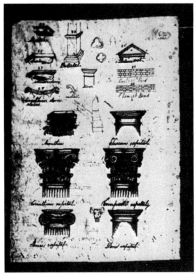

FIGURE 2　A page from "Civil Architecture, 1873"

FIGURE 3　Barber's "Nail Holding Attachment for Hammers," 1884

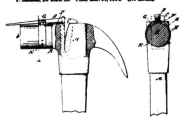

FIGURE 4　The Congregational Church, De Kalb, Illinois, 1885–8

FIGURE 5 Washington Avenue,
Knoxville, c. 1890

FIGURE 6 *The Cottage Souvenir,*
Eighteen Engravings of Houses . . .
c. 1887

FIGURE 7 *Modern Artistic Cottages, or*
the Cottage Souvenir . . . c. 1888

to work trying to establish his practice, engaging in various business relationships before settling upon J. C. White as his business manager in 1892.[13] White, active in the suburban residential development of northeast Knoxville, was a principal of the Edgewood Land Improvement Company, whose interests centered on Washington Avenue.[14] Thus it should be no surprise that in this neighborhood could be found a number of residences designed by the Barber firm: in fact *The Cottage Souvenir No. 2* includes both J. C. White's home, as Design No. 54, and Barber's first home in Knoxville, as Design No. 60.

Although there seems to be no record of exactly when Barber first thought of publishing his designs, his first known works were produced before he moved to Knoxville. *The Cottage Souvenir, Eighteen Engravings of Houses Ranging in Price from $900.00 to $8000.00 in Wood, Brick and Stone, Artistically Combined* was published in De Kalb in 1887 or early 1888.[15] The collection was simply presented: the designs were printed on card stock 6¾″ high by 5¼″ wide, with an elevation or perspective on the front and plans on the back. The "binding" was merely a piece of yarn, threaded through a hole punched in the corner of each card, and tied in a bow. This was, in fact, an illustrated sampler intended to advertise Barber's capabilities.

More designs were added to this first collection in a staple-bound fifty-six page booklet, entitled *Modern Artistic Cottages, or the Cottage Souvenir, Designed to Meet the Wants of Mechanics and Home Builders*, probably also printed in De Kalb, about 1888.[16] For $.85 the purchaser received twenty-five different designs, introduced by three pages of "Brief Hints to Home Builders;" the reader was invited to correspond with the author, who would provide all the necessary plans and specifications. This marked, on a modest and informal basis, Barber's entry into an architectural practice which would rely upon correspondence rather than direct contact between the prospective homeowner and the architect. Barber was not, however, the first to employ this method of practice on a widespread basis. That claim belongs to George Palliser, a builder-architect of Bridgeport, Connecticut, who, in 1876, had begun a string of over twenty publications.[17] One of these, as was mentioned earlier, had been purchased by Barber while he was still in Kansas.

Perhaps owing to the rather stiff hold which more established architects had in Knoxville, it was some time before any of Barber's larger domestic designs were constructed locally. In any event, it was upon moving to the South that Barber placed an increased emphasis upon the mail-order aspect of his architectural practice. This can be seen in *The Cottage Souvenir No. 2, A Repository of Artistic Cottage Architecture and Miscellaneous Designs*, copyrighted in December 1890. Much larger in size and more diverse in content than either of Barber's previous works, it includes not only most of the designs published earlier but also a number of others, many of which had been recently completed, as is illustrated by the incorporation of photographs. While it is primarily a catalogue of 59 designs for cottages and houses costing from $500 to $8,000, the book also contains schemes for several barns, a chapel, a church, two store fronts, and two summer pavilions, as well as 25 pages of interior and exterior details. The volume concludes with a schedule of prices of materials and labor used in the estimates, and with a price list of working plans and specifications. Available for $2.75 clothbound or $2.00 in paperback, *The Cottage Souvenir No. 2* was the first of Barber's publications to receive widespread attention and marks the beginning of his mail-order architectural practice on a nation-wide basis.

Thereafter, Barber continued to publish large, mail-order catalogues as well as a series of samplers—nine in all.[18] In addition, he produced the eighty-six page booklet entitled *Appreciation*,[19] a compilation of the testimonials of satisfied customers, letters of thanks, plans of buildings, and "mug shots" of proud new owners. This provides some insight as to the kind of people who were purchasing designs from Barber. These were members of the rising middle class: the vice president of a small town bank, the railroad company treasurer, the hardware company executive, the young attorney or doctor, or perhaps the oyster packer and planter.

A more ambitious undertaking, and one which undoubtedly furthered Barber's practice, was his monthly magazine, *American Homes. A Journal Devoted to Planning, Building and Beautifying the Home*, begun in January 1895.[20] Just as Barber had borrowed his method of practice from Palliser, he likewise followed another of Palliser's imitators, Robert W. Shoppell of New York City,[21] in producing a periodical designed to educate the public and support the mail-order approach. It is likely that Barber was aware of *Shoppell's Modern Houses*, but he attempted to capture a somewhat wider audience by assembling more than a simple portfolio of sketches. While *American Homes* did, in part, present the Barber Company's latest and most popular designs, from its earliest issues the journal was quite literary, placing great emphasis on the Colonial heritage of America and discussing at length the major, patriotic landmarks of the country. A typical issue might contain an article on the cost of residental construction by the Omaha builder and prolific writer Isaac Perry Hicks; an article on the proper siting of a suburban home and the landscaping of its lot; and an account of a visit to a current ex-

FIGURE 8 Barber's later mail-order catalogues.

FIGURE 9 *Appreciation*, a compilation of testimonials

FIGURE 10 *American Homes*, I, No. I
(January, 1895) Cover

FIGURE 11 A typical advertisement

position. The history of architecture was reviewed in a series of articles by the Louisville architect Charles Hite-Smith. By January 1899, *American Homes* was concerned as much with suburban life in general—with articles on furniture, drapery, gardening, poetry, and serialized romances—as it was involved with domestic architecture, likely in an effort to broaden popular appeal.[22] Barber remained in control of the magazine until 1902, when the editorial offices moved to New York City; thereafter he served as an occasional contributor.

The idea behind all the catalogues—including *The Cottage Souvenir No. 2*—and *American Homes* was to induce in the reader the desire for a new home designed by George F. Barber and Company. Having seen an advertisement in either a trade periodical, a popular literary or women's magazine,[23] or perhaps having obtained a copy of *American Homes*, the reader became a prospective client as he sent in his name and address with his check to purchase a catalogue. This, in turn, outlined the procedure the client would follow to secure all the necessary scale plans and elevations, full size details, blank contract forms, a sheet of color samples, and a bill of materials. In *The Cottage Souvenir No. 2*, for example, the client might simply choose one of the designs presented and, after consulting the price list on page 168, order a set of construction documents. If only slight changes in the drawings were needed,

Barber urged they be negotiated between client and builder. If, however, greater alterations were desired, the Barber firm would provide them at a moderate cost. "Write to us concerning any changes wanted in plans, and keep writing till you get what you want. Don't be afraid of writing too often. We are not easily offended." [24]

By 1892, Barber's analysis of such correspondence between the client and his office led to the adoption of an order form to ensure more satisfactory results. By filling in the blanks of a questionnaire and sketching a rough floor plan, the client would greatly expedite the mail-order process. In fact, by the end of the decade, not only had the questionnaire become more detailed, but its reverse side was used as a "Handy Sketch Sheet," ruled off in $\frac{1}{8}$" squares, for the convenience of all concerned. However, in all of his catalogues, Barber continued to offer the client the option of an individually designed house, not one based solely on a published design, but developed through extensive correspondence between client and architect. Thus, Barber's books were not mere portfolios, but were in fact mail-order catalogues that were a part of a continually improving process of providing custom-designed houses.

With increased advertising in the mid-1890s, the demand for "Barber Houses" expanded, extending even beyond this country. The firm grew accordingly, gradually taking up an entire floor of the French and Roberts Building, it too, designed by Barber. By 1900, George F. Barber and Company, Architects, was the largest architectural office in Knoxville, and quite probably in Tennessee, employing as many as thirty draftsmen and about twenty secretaries. Most of the draftsmen were relatively inexperienced: whether a former postman or a recent high school graduate, most were hired to copy the more than eight hundred designs produced by the firm.[25] A few, however, such as Barber's distant relative, Charles W. Barrett, did go on to establish practices of their own.[26]

FIGURE 12   The Questionnaire of the Barber Company, 1892

FIGURE 13, A AND B   The Questionnaire improved and "Handy Sketch Sheet," 1898

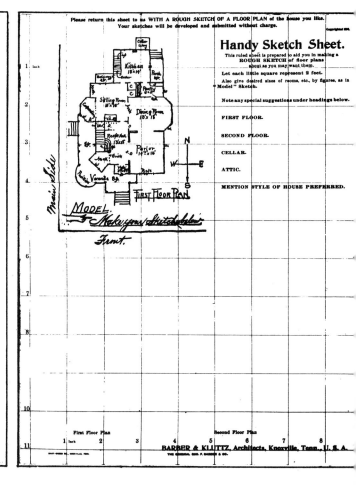

FIGURE 14　A drafting room in the French and Roberts Building, Knoxville, c. 1896

Given the number of buildings for which Barber's office was responsible, and the mail-order method that was employed, it is not surprising that designs produced for one client would be used with but minor alterations for another. Thus, to anyone who has seen more than one example of the same design, the question invariably arises as to what degree these houses were prefabricated. This question must be answered very carefully. It is true that most of the elements (staircases, windows and doors and their frames) as well as the materials for construction could be shipped in crates by railroad to relatively remote areas. This practiee, however, was not uncommon in the late nineteenth century nor does it, in itself, constitute prefabrication. There is no evidence that any member of Barber's firm was programmatically involved with a millwork company, although building component manufacturers who advertised in his publications were recommended to clients.[27] Barber's statements with regard to the construction of his designs are clear.

Knowing as I do, that my working drawings, when they leave the office, go out of reach of my personal supervision, I have taken especial pains to make everything plain and easily understood by mechanics generally. Every detail that goes from this office is full size and drawn by hand (not printed).
Everything requiring it has a detail given, and they are all ready to be pricked off on the material for working out.[28]

Barber prided himself on the accuracy with which a reasonably competent local builder could work from his drawings and specifications. Only on occasion, with a more elaborate design or in a particularly remote area did he or a member of his firm supervise construction. Measurements taken on different buildings of specific details which at first glance appear identical repeatedly reveal considerable differences in craftmanship. (PLATES 1–6)

　　Barber's own ideas on the need for the mail-order process were set forth in an editorial he wrote for *American Homes* in February 1898:

In many localities there are no architects at hand who may be readily consulted; out of this condition has grown a business of supplying such clients through the mails, and the development of this method has been rapid. Thousands of such plans are annually made, and sent through the mails or by express, and where the business has been systematized so that the clients' wishes are understood by the architect the result has been quite as satisfactory as if personal consultation has been held.[29]

FIGURE 15   The subdivision of "Normandy Heights," outside Baltimore, c. 1896

Certainly thousands of plans were made—perhaps as many as 20,000 sets by Barber's firm alone over the course of the nearly two decades he was in practice.[30] How successful Barber's publications became can be judged not only by the hundreds of residential buildings which are noted in the Company's literature—forty-seven were erected by one developer in Baltimore—but also by the geographical distribution of letters and thanks which have survived. Correspondence came from as far away as Japan, China and the Philippines, as well as from South Africa and Europe, in addition to letters from almost every state of the Union and several provinces in Canada.

Having reviewed the number of Barber's publications, the method in which they were used and their success, there remains the question of their design content. *The Cottage Souvenir No. 2* is extremely instructive in this regard, for it demonstrates Barber's eclectic approach to design and his talents in composition and decoration, beginning with his introductory remarks on the "Principles of Design, Harmony of Form and Proportion in Architecture."

Barber's earliest published designs, which he notes as variants of the Queen Anne mode, were quite obviously in imitation of the high-style architecture he had observed as well as what he had studied in the pattern-books he had purchased, and, more important, what he may have seen in contemporary building journals. A house such as Design No. 28 or Design No. 41 in *The Cottage Souvenir No. 2*, the latter built in late 1887 for Charles E. Bradt of De Kalb, was not exceptionally creative, but it was respectable enough to be featured in the March 1888 issue of *Carpentry and Building*.[31] For Mr. Bradt, Barber designed a multi-gabled, asymmetrical form whose exterior displayed the full complement of woodworking treatments at his disposal: weather-boards, vertical and diagonal novelty boards, fish-scale shingles, brackets, and gable ornaments. Whether one employed the slightly more compact "Northern" plan developed in De Kalb, or the more extended "Southern" scheme with its extra porch, apparently used in Beaumont, Texas, the arrangement of the hall and front rooms did not vary. This allowed the front elevation to remain the same.

Even more attention, however, was paid to the fronts of designs which Barber termed "Romanesque." Examples such as No. 55 in *The Cottage Souvenir No. 2* built for J. H. Setchel in Cuba, New York, (PLATE 7) and No. 562 in *Art in Architecture* built for Isaac B. Zeigler of Knoxville, Tennessee, C. S. Craig of Richland Center, Wisconsin, (PLATES 8, 9) and William Ackerman of Mount Vernon, Ohio, were seen as expressions of the style common in many governmental, institutional and religious buildings: the Richardsonian Romanesque. In brick and stone the forms of this style were easily understood, but there was little precedent to guide Barber and others who translated the color and texture of these materials into this country's most convenient material—wood.[32]

FIGURE 16   Design No. 562 in *Art in Architecture*, "Romanesque"

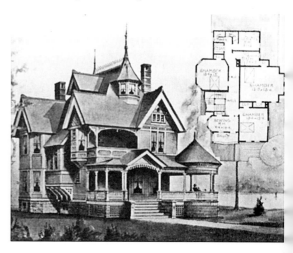

FIGURE 17   Elevation, Design No. 55, in *The Cottage Souvenir No. 2*

FIGURE 18   Design No. 27, *The Cottage Souvenir, Revised and Enlarged* (1892)

Barber's most creative efforts were directed toward this translation. "Romanesque" elements were added to enrich the Queen Anne front. An engaged tower or turret, either round or octagonal, became the dominant element of the design. This was placed off center, often between the two major facades of the house, especially if it was to be built on a corner lot. An oriel window might be added, usually projecting from a second story corner, to complement the picturesque outline. Open, circular pavilions were constructed, somewhat detached from the house, at the corner of the veranda. Perhaps most distinctive, though they have rarely survived, were the Syrian arches—distant relatives of those Richardson made famous—great yawning curves of lattice-like bead screening which partially hid the off-center entrances behind.

A few of Barber's designs cannot be categorized as simply Queen Anne or Romanesque. These compositions, such as Design No. 36 in *The Cottage Souvenir No. 2* constructed in Madisonville, Kentucky, and Mt. Dora, Florida, (PLATES 10,11) or Design No. 27 in *The Cottage Souvenir, Revised and Enlarged* (1892) constructed in Calvert, Texas, Alameda, California, (PLATES 12, 16) and Eau Claire, Wisconsin, all were "unique" eclectic designs. Intersecting, multifaceted forms, with inset porches and projecting bays, replete with such details as buttressed, panelled and capped chimneys with inset sash, keyhole windows, and spool-like columns, were employed to declare their owner's distinction and help secure his place in the community. Even today, one must look with wonder at such an involved design as the W. C. Arthurs House in Mount Vernon, Illinois, and its sisters, the J. A. Beck House in Fairfield, Iowa, and the J. W. Truesdell House in Syracuse, New York. (PLATES 13, 14, 15)

The Cottage Souvenir No. 2 does not show any of Barber's Colonial designs, which he first published in 1893. In general, Barber left the Romanesque style only very reluctantly, retaining much of its form, massing and arrangement of rooms in the mode he termed the "Colonial Renaissance." Designs such as No. 70G in *Modern Dwellings*, built for J. W. Chamberlain of Akron, Ohio, about 1900, owed their early American association to the use of shingles and perhaps some "neo-Adamesque" detailing. Their Renaissance connection derived only from the porch columns and the scrolled modillions under the eaves. In the Colonial Renaissance, as in the Queen Anne and Romanesque, Barber's stylistic terminology was almost entirely dependent upon the minor elements which were added and reinterpreted, and not on the exact duplication of an historical model.

FIGURE 19   Design No. 70G, *Modern Dwellings* (1898)

FIGURE 20   FIGURE 21

FIGURE 24

FIGURE 22   FIGURE 23

A more clearly understood Colonial mode, yet still picturesque in character, was one derived from New England, the shingled "Colonial Cottage." This was a style which Barber "imported," probably inspired by examples in architectural periodicals. To the casual observer, such a cottage often suggested that it was but a single story in height, though actually it was two. The second floor, "hidden" beneath the gambrel, the flared gable, or the more fashionable hipped roof, was lit by a few dormers and, perhaps, a Palladian window in the gable. Such designs as No. 551 or No. 552 in *Art in Architecture*, the latter built for Barber himself in Knoxville about 1895, illustrate the type although there are almost innumerable variations.

The "Colonial House," by comparison, was almost always a structure overtly two stories high. This was the "square Colonial home" whose chief attributes were "simplicity of design and good proportion," constructed with the idea of gaining the most for one's investment. In general, this meant a square plan and a nearly symmetrical front. Designs such as No. 772 and No. 773 in *Modern American Homes* are not unlike many dwellings designed for speculative construction.

Much as the Queen Anne was upstaged by the Romanesque, these three Colonial modes were outstripped by the "Georgian" or "Classic Colonial" style, employed in Barber's most pretentious designs. The "Classic Colonial" residence often stood on a podium or base and boasted one or more projecting porticoes of coupled columns, generally of the colossal order. In some of the more complex examples a single story porch was woven into the portico and across the width of the house. Behind the columns was likely a symmetrical facade of salmon-colored brick with stone trim or, if executed in wood, horizontal boarding, painted white. A hipped roof rose from the cornice to a flat deck crowned by a balustrade. Balanced dormers and flanking chimneys completed the composition. Such residences as that built for C. L. Post, celebrated cereal food manufacturer in Battle Creek, Michigan, N. E. Graham, President of the Peoples Bank, in East Brady, Pennsylvania, or the more simplified design built for sawmill owner J. B. Galloway in Clarendon, Arkansas, (PLATES 17, 18) give some indication of what was possible given the mail-order method and a liberal budget in the early twentieth century.

Designs in the "mission style," the "English half-timbered," the "bungalo," and the "Craftsman" were inserted in the firm's later catalogues, although comparatively few were actually built. (PLATE 19) Increasingly occupied with local construction, by 1908 the mail-order architectural practice of the company was suspended. Moreover, when George's son, Charles Ives Barber, returned from his

FIGURE 26 Design No. 775, *Art in Architecture* (1902–1903)

architectural studies at the University of Pennsylvania in 1910, he brought new ideas to his father's firm. Having absorbed both the Beaux Arts preferences in design and its attendant emphasis upon the architect as a professional, Charles had little sympathy for either his father's stylistic tastes or his manner of practice. Nevertheless, when George F. Barber died, on February 17, 1915,[33] he was mourned as an architect of considerable importance and influence.

As a carpenter, architect and publisher, George Franklin Barber was, perhaps, a little more than typical of his time. Having grown up in the Midwest, he had observed the arrival of the first mail-order catalogues, and he knew their importance to small town residents and rural settlers. Just as his knowledge of architecture had been acquired through books, ordered by mail, so too his practice was based on catalogues—such as *The Cottage Souvenir No. 2*. This was significant as the first of his many publications to receive nationwide attention. As it demonstrates, he was a talented designer, although his designs rode closer to the crest of popular opinion than before it. Thus, George Franklin Barber was not only an exemplar of the rising middle class of the era, but, more important, he helped to convey, solidify and then materialize the American ideals of comfort and artistic taste.

MICHAEL A. TOMLAN
Ithaca, New York
June 1981

NOTES

1 "How Will You Build?" *American Homes. A Journal Devoted to Planning, Building and Beautifying the Home*, IV, No. 2 (February 1898), p. 50.

2 The reference to "Barber Houses" is historically justifiable; see " 'Barber' Houses," *American Homes*, IX, No. 10 (October 1899), p. 225.

3 David West Barber, "Happy Memories" (Knoxville, Tennessee: Unpublished typescript, 1972), n.p. This and the "Geneology of the Barber Family" in the Barber family Bible provide the basic biographical information contained in this study. The author would like to express his appreciation to Mrs. Charles Ives Barber and to the late David West Barber, architect, both of Knoxville, Tennessee, for their cooperation in collecting information on the Barber family in 1972 and 1973. Subsequently, Mrs. Charles C. Hunt, Librarian, of De Kalb, Illinois, and Mrs. J. R. Prichard, Historian, of Fort Scott, Kansas, were quite helpful on visits to their respective cities. Space limitations prevent listing all the owners, both past and present, who have so patiently answered my inquiries regarding their "Barber Houses," but their cooperation as well as that provided by several public librarians has been invaluable. Acknowledgement should also be made of a Robert James Eidlitz Travelling Fellowship awarded by the College of Architecture, Art and Planning at Cornell University in 1976 for the extensive field research which underlies this study. Lastly, my thanks go to Craig Leonard, preservation consultant, of Bluffton, Indiana, who so generously loaned his rare, original copy of *The Cottage Souvenir No. 2* for reproduction.

4 Letter, George F. Barber, Marmaton, Kansas, to Manley DeWitt Barber, January 25 [1870]. Private Collection.

5 Warranty Deed, William Barrett and Wife to George F. Barber, filed May 8, 1878; Book 24, page 585, Bourbon County, Kansas. Private Collection. This corresponds with maps in the *Illustrated Historical Atlas of Bourbon Co., Kansas* (Philadelphia: Edwards Bros., 1878), p. 13 and p. 29. It should be noted that many horticulturists and seedsmen had already perfected their mail-order business by this time.

6 Tax Assessment Receipts, Bourbon County, Kansas, 1878–1880. Private Collection.

7 David West Barber, private interview, June 17, 1973. "West" Barber had both a personal and professional relationship with George F. Barber, for the latter was not only his uncle, but also his first employer.

8 William T. Comstock joined Amos J. Bicknell's firm in May 1877, became a partner in January 1879, and assumed full control of the business in May 1881. Comstock did not use a stamp to identify the books he sold, but he did carry a full line of the Pallisers' publications.

9 David West Barber, "Happy Memories."

10 "Specifications, Patent Number 20013," filed with the Canadian Patent Office, Ottawa, Canada, August 16, 1884, p. 4. The same device was patented in the United States slightly earlier: U. S. Patent Number 299, 717, filed March 31, 1884.

11 See, for example, the *Inland Architect and News Record*, IX, No. 10 (July 1887), p. 100, and XI, No. 8 (July 1888), p. 91; also *The De Kalb Review*, April 21, 1887, p. 4.

12 *The De Kalb Review*, February 2, 1888, p. 4.

FIGURE 27   The bookstamp of A. J. Bicknell & Co., 1876

13 Short-lived partnerships with Martin E. Parmalee, an architect from Minnesota, and with Charles T. Mould, a business manager, both apparently proved unsatisfactory. Barber first became acquainted with White when asked to design his house in Spring 1890. See "Plans and Plan-Making," *American Homes*, II, No. 1 (January 1896), p. 22. About 1895, White was replaced as Barber's partner by the architect Thomas A. Kluttz, of Georgia.

14 *Map of Knoxville* (Knoxville, Tennessee: Ogden Bros. & Co., 1895), n.p.

15 This may have been issued more than once by Tyrell & Fay, Printers, of De Kalb.

16 This, too, seems to have been issued at least twice, judging from differences in the few surviving copies.

17 Michael A. Tomlan, "The Palliser Brothers and Their Publications," an introduction to *The Palliser's Late Victorian Architecture* [sic], a facsimile of George and Charles Palliser's *Model Homes* (1878) and *American Cottage Homes* (1878), as republished in 1888 under the title *American Architecture*, and *New Cottage Homes and Details* (1887). (Watkins Glen, New York: The American Life Foundation and Study Institute, 1978), p. [iii–vii].

18 In addition to the three works mentioned, the following titles are known:

> George F. Barber, *The Cottage Souvenir, Revised and Enlarged, Containing Over Two Hundred Original Designs and Plans of Artistic Dwellings* (Knoxville, Tenn.: S. B. Newman & Co., 1892).
>
> —————, *New Model Dwellings and How Best to Build Them. Containing a Great Variety of Designs, Plans and Interior Views of Modern Dwellings Together with a Large Amount of Valuable Information Indispensible to those who Contemplate Building* (Knoxville, Tenn.: G. F. Barber & Co., 1893).
>
> George F. Barber & Co., *Artistic Homes, How to Plan and How to Build Them* (Knoxville, Tenn.: S. B. Newman & Co., 1895).
>
> —————, *Artistic Homes, How to Plan and How to Build Them, No. 2* (Knoxville, Tenn.: S. B. Newman & Co., 1895).
>
> —————, *Artistic Homes, How to Plan and How to Build Them, No. 3* (Knoxville, Tenn.: S. B. Newman & Co., 1896).
>
> —————, *Homes and Barns for Village or Farm* (Knoxville, Tenn.: S. B. Newman & Co., 1898).
>
> —————, *Modern Dwellings, a Book of Practical Designs and Plans for Those who Wish to Build or Beautify Their Homes* (Knoxville, Tenn.: S. B. Newman & Co., [Nine editions known, yearly] 1898–1907).
>
> Geo. F. Barber, *Art in Architecture, with the Modern Architectural Designer, For those who Wish to Build or Beautify Their Homes* (Knoxville, Tenn.: S. B. Newman & Co., Second Edition, 1902–03).
>
> —————, *Modern American Homes, a Book of Everything for Those who are Planning to Build or Beautify Their Homes* (Knoxville, Tenn.: Gaut-Ogden Co., [Five editions known, yearly] 1903–07).

19 George F. Barber & Co., *Appreciation* (Knoxville, Tenn.: S. B. Newman & Co., [1896]).

20 George F. Barber & Co., *American Homes. A Journal Devoted to Planning, Building and Beautifying the Home* (Knoxville, Tenn.: American Homes Publishing Company, 1895–1901; New York: The Hite-Smith Publishing Company, 1902–04).

21 Robert W. Shoppell of New York City was probably the first to openly mimic Palliser's method of mail-order practice. A dealer in publishing supplies and woodcuts, Shoppell began to organize his Cooperative Building Plan Association about 1880, and assembled some of his collection of miscellaneous illustrations into a paperback booklet entitled *How to Build a House: Cooperative Building Plans, Containing the Most Approved Designs for Villas, Cottages, Farm Houses, and Suburban Architecture*, published in April 1883. Shoppell was the first to undertake a journal specifically to forward his mail-order business, with *Shoppell's Modern Houses, an Illustrated Architectural Quarterly,* begun in January 1886.

22 Thus, *American Homes* acquired various aspects of contemporary women's magazines as, for example, the *Woman's Home Companion* and the immensely popular *Ladies' Home Journal*. While the circulation of Barber's magazine, which was about 9500 at the turn of the century, could in no way compare with the giants in this class, it did approach the popularity of *Shoppell's Modern Houses*, which was producing approximately 10,000 copies per issue.

23 *The Manufacturer and Builder, Scribner's, The Century, The Churchman, Woman's Home Companion*, and *Ladies Home Journal*—to name a few—all carried the advertisements of the Barber Company.

24 George F. Barber, *The Cottage Souvenir No. 2, A Repository of Artistic Cottage Architecture and Miscellaneous Designs* (Knoxville, Tenn.: S. B. Newman & Co., 1891), p. 9.

25 "Plans and Plan-Making," *American Homes*, II, No. 1 (January 1896), pp. 22–25.

26 Charles W. Barrett subsequently established an architectural partnership in Raleigh, North Carolina which, for a time, made use of the mail-order method to supplement his practice.

27 This was particularly true after 1895. Circulars addressed to potential advertisers survive, claiming "YOU CAN HAVE YOUR GOODS SPECIFIED equally with others who are Advertisers in *American Homes* by placing your advertisement in it."

28 George F. Barber, *The Cottage Souvenir No. 2*, pp. 10–11.

29 "How Will You Build?" *American Homes*, p. 50.

30 This figure is derived from the fact that Barber's mail-order practice lasted from 1888 to 1908, and the claim, stated in the advertising circular mentioned above, that "This firm makes from 700 to 1000 sets of Plans for Buildings each year." However, a total of 20,000 sets of plans is probably a somewhat conservative estimate. At least one reference, in the introduction to *New Model Dwellings and How Best to Build Them*, published in 1893, stated that "The designs and plans shown in this work are the choice selections from some 6,000 to 8,000 prepared in our office during the past three years. . . ."

31 "House Design," *Carpentry and Building*, X, No. 3 (March 1888), pp. 50–54, continued in X, No. 4 (April 1888), pp. 76–77.

32 This has yet to be fully recognized by most architectural historians and preservationists. In *American Homes*, Barber's references are even clearer, for he includes photographs of Richardson's buildings.

33 *Knoxville Journal and Tribune*, February 18, 1915, p. 4.

PLATE 1 "Front Elevation" *American Homes*, I. No. 1, (January 1895) p. 31. (Photograph: Courtesy of the Boston Public Library)

PLATE 3 C. M. Shepard Residence, Mobile, Alabama, 1897. (Photograph: Courtesy of Mrs. Lee McCoy, former owner)

PLATE 2 W. J. Greenman Residence, Cortland, New York, 1895. (Photograph: M. A. Tomlan)

PLATE 4 W. Dawes Residence, Johnstown, New York, 1894. (Photograph: M. A. Tomlan)

PLATE 3

PLATE 4

PLATE 5 L. J. Hodge Residence,
Wenona, Illinois, c. 1893. (Photograph:
M. A. Tomlan)

PLATE 6 I. W. P. Buchanan Residence,
Lebanon, Tennessee, 1897. (Photograph:
M. A. Tomlan)

PLATE 7   J. H. Setchel Residence, Cuba,
New York, 1888. (Photograph: M. A.
Tomlan)

PLATE 8   I. B. Ziegler Residence,
Knoxville, Tennessee, 1892. (Photograph:
M. A. Tomlan)

PLATE 9   C. S. Craig Residence,
Richland Center, Wisconsin, c. 1892.
(Photograph: M. A. Tomlan)

PLATE 10   J. B. Harvey Residence, Madisonville, Kentucky, c. 1895. (Photograph: Courtesy of Mr. and Mrs. J. W. Bassett, owners)

PLATE 11   J. P. Donnelly Residence, Mt. Dora, Florida, 1893. (Photograph: Courtesy of Diane Greer and Dan Deibler, Florida Division of Archives, History and Records Management, Florida Department of State, Tallahassee, Florida)

PLATE 12   L. Parish Residence, Calvert,
Texas, c. 1893. (Photograph: M. A.
Tomlan)

PLATE 13 W. C. Arthurs Residence, Mt.
Vernon, Illinois, 1895. (Photograph:
M. A. Tomlan)

PLATE 14 J. A. Beck Residence,
Fairfield, Iowa, 1896. (Photograph:
M. A. Tomlan)

PLATE 15   J. W. Truesdell Residence, Syracuse, New York, c. 1895. (Photograph: M. A. Tomlan)

PLATE 16   D. Brehaut Residence, Alameda, California, 1893. (Photograph: Courtesy Elizabeth Hancock Sillin, Western Regional Office, National Trust for Historic Preservation, San Francisco, California)

PLATE 17   N. E. Graham Residence,
East Brady, Pennsylvania, c. 1897.
(Photograph: George F. Barber *Modern
Dwellings. A Book of Practical Designs
and Plans for Those Who Wish to Build
or Beautify Their Homes*, [Knoxville,
Tennessee: S. B. Newman & Co., 1898]
p. 31)

PLATE 18   J. B. Galloway Residence,
Clarendon, Arkansas, designed in 1906,
constructed in 1910. (Photograph:
Courtesy of Ethel S. Goodstein, Historic
Preservation Program, Arkansas
Department of Natural and Cultural
Heritage, Little Rock, Arkansas)

PLATE 19   S. F. Sherman Residence,
Newark, New York, 1906–1907.
(Photograph: M. A. Tomlan)

PLATE 20   F. W. Spinning Block,
Richmond, Indiana, 1895. (Photograph:
M. A. Tomlan) This is a combination of
Design No. 67 and Design No. 68 in
The Cottage Souvenir No. 2

The Cottage

SOUVENIR

No. 2.

A Repository of

Artistic Cottage Architecture

* AND Miscellaneous Designs. *

OVER 50 DESIGNS

OF MODERN COTTAGES,

COSTING FROM $400 TO $8000

BY Geo. F. Barber,
ARCHITECT.

REMARKS

ON THE

Principles of Design, Harmony of Form and Proportion in Architecture.

NATURE, in all her wondrous productions, has faithfully and accurately adhered to the Divine law of harmony, both in form and true proportions of parts. In no place should there be a closer adherence to the fundamental principles nature has laid down for us than in the design and construction of our houses.

A perfect house should look as if it had grown where nature intended it should, and in strict accordance with her perfect laws. It should be as finely and accurately finished in every part as a nicely proportioned and handsomely designed piece of furniture. It should not have that shabby and unfinished appearance so common with our present style of structures. It is just as easy and just as cheap for a builder to erect a well proportioned and handsomely designed house—if the plans call for it—as to construct one of faulty and ungainly appearance.

A man will look at an elegant house, or a drawing of it, and remark dubiously: "I cannot possibly afford such a costly house as that. I must build on a cheaper plan." He does not know that it is the style and proportions of a house that give it the appearance of costliness, while in reality it costs no more than the shabby, ill-proportioned structure he contemplates building.

A perfectly and handsomely designed house or cottage has the appearance of costing from one hundred to several thousand dollars more than it in reality costs, while a poorly formed cottage, where no taste has been displayed either in design or construction, shows exactly the reverse. It is plainly observable then, that a tasty, finely constructed building, though costing a trifle more than an ordinary, commonplace affair, is of far greater value to the owner, raising the price of his property, and causing it to sell more readily, also enhancing the value of property in the neighborhood.

In building, do not get the poorest mechanic (i. e. a poor workman) that you can find, simply because he will work cheap. It is poor economy, as poor workmanship is always expensive.

A house is something you will either enjoy or be disgusted with as long perhaps as you live. Then do not slight or leave out a single thing that is necessary to make a perfect home. Its proportions may be small, but with its outer and inner appointments in perfect harmony of style, it will be a palace of beauty and elegance.

Before you begin to build, be sure you have secured the very best plan and design that you can obtain for the price. Correspond with architects and designers until you have found just what you want. Do not be afraid of offending some one. When you have secured your plans and perfected your details, get the best mechanic you can find to do the work. Not the *cheapest*, but the *best*, as you would call in the best physician in case you were seriously ill, or the most trusty surgeon if dangerously wounded. Mechanics generally seem to forget that the chief object of a dwelling is the comfort and convenience of its occupants.

A few more words in regard to true proportion and harmony of form as applied to architecture.

We will give you an example.

In music we must have harmony of tone. This is music. But to add to the sweetness of this harmony we must have perfect time. This gives to music dignity. But to still add to this we must have expression, which every one understands in music is its life.

Harmony is as essential in color and form as in music. Proportion in a building consists in having its dimensions or body parts in perfect relation to each other, the length to the breadth, and these to the height. They must all be happily proportioned, and the roof—the most important part of the whole structure—should have its height, steepness of pitch, projection of cornice, and its broken outline against the sky, thoroughly studied and most carefully arranged.

Towers, verandas and bay windows are all large parts of the design, and should be in such exact proportion with the rest of the building, that it would seem impossible to dispense with either one of them without injuring the effect of the entire structure.

Proportion is to architecture what harmony is to music—the first thing to be considered, without which all else is a failure.

We can have music in harmony of tone, without time. So we can have a house of elegant appearance if properly proportioned, without ornamentation.

Ornamentation is the same to architecture as time is to music. It gives to its already handsome proportions, life, expression and dignity that it could not possibly have without it. But this ornamentation must be properly applied—applied in a finer sense of the word *proportion* than has been considered necessary in the structural part of the design.

Each ornament must in itself be a proportional gem, and they equally and artistically distributed over the entire structure, not crowded or jammed into clusters to be unsightly or unmeaning in their positions. There is, perhaps, more skill or tact required in arranging ornamental work properly than in any other part of the design. Each tiny ornament should peek out at you from its allotted position on the building with all the dignity and importance of its absolute necessity in the make up of the structure; a necessity as imperative as that of a letter in forming the completeness of a word.

How many houses do we see around us with their ornaments nailed about them in the most unsightly and inartistic manner imaginable? This is not architecture. The beauty of the structure is ruined by such defacement.

A bracket under the corner of an overhanging roof or other place where weight is supposed to come, should appear to be exactly equal to the occasion—that of holding the load with all ease—not to look as if it was straining itself to bear up under the mighty burden, nor as if its footing was insecure, presenting the appearance of constantly trying to hold itself in position. This appearance gives the observer from below a tired and uneasy feeling, being anxious to relieve the support from its unnatural position.

If every feature of the structure is properly proportioned, the observer will be led to exclaim:

"What a beautiful structure!" without even knowing why it is so.

The next important feature necessary in the principles of good designing is harmony of form. This, as applied to the finished structure, is the same as expression in music.

Expression is applied to music to give it a fine quality and a perfection of grace and beauty that shall be so complete in itself, that nothing farther can be added for its improvement.

Harmony of form is to be applied almost exclusively to the ornamental details of the design. What we mean by harmony of form is the naturally graceful relation curved and straight lines bear to each other, where they come in contact.

It is of the utmost importance that these principles should be thoroughly known and understood by the designer, or the best results will not be attained.

In the contour or outline of detail ornament, is where this principle of harmony of form is of the most importance.

[The placing of these ornaments upon the building after they are made, comes under the head of proportion.]

The outlines of brackets, for instance, must have their curved and straight lines so related to each other as to appear restful and pleasing to the untrained eye.

It is impossible in so small a space to give any examples or practical lessons on this important branch of the subject.

The subjects under discussion are natural principles, and are as mathematically true as any branch of mathematics, and in order that the designer may be master of them, he must be created with a talent for such things. How many times have we seen an architect trying to design a scroll, with only the most unsatisfactory results.

We have spoken of design—but what is design? It is, in one sense of the word, the materialization of a thought, or a train of thoughts; a premeditation—something thought of and then worked out.

We have seen architects, when wanting a design for a bracket or scroll, find the dimensions, place the pencil on the paper at the desired point, and push it across the sheet in an irregular, zigzag line that was totally unmeaning in character. Yet it was called a design and admired as such.

This is where we get so many of our poor designs. They are carelessly drawn, without the least knowledge of the true principles of designing.

Carpenters are usually careless in their methods of designing, and that is why there is such a vast difference between their designs and those of a trained and careful architect. The works of the former are lacking in the true principles of grace and beauty that are everywhere so noticeable in those of the latter.

An architect must be a production of nature, in order to be successful in the truest sense of the word.

Bear this in mind: A beautiful and correctly proportioned house will cost you no more, if you start right, than an unsightly, illy-proportioned one. All that is necessary is to choose between a practical architect and a bungler. If a $30.00 suit of clothes fits you with faultless precision, you are much better satisfied with it than you would be with an ungainly, ill-fitting suit at the same price. The same may be said in regard to architecture.

There is no excuse for building an ungainly, shabbily proportioned edifice. Go at the work in the proper manner. Secure the best designer, pay him his price, get the best workmen, and enjoy the perfection they have called forth by their united efforts, with a contented and happy heart.

The musician who can arrange the musical octave upon the staff in the best relation for the most perfect harmony, has succeeded in producing the sweetest and most exquisite music. The designer, likewise, who can arrange lines in the most perfect manner relative to each other as required by the true laws of harmony of form, has succeeded in producing the finest and most perfect object in his class of studies—a building ever attractive to the eye of the beholder, ever new and pleasing, and instead of growing old and unsightly by constant association, it will call forth fresh emotions of admiration at every recurring visit.

A building lacking in the true principles of harmony and proportion will become tiresome and uninviting by age.

In regard to the planning of houses for the different sections of country, I wish to say that I have had several years of personal practice in the West, and especially in the North, in the vicinity of Chicago, and have lately had two years experience in traveling over the South, from the Ohio River to the Gulf of Mexico, planning, arranging and designing residences for every class of people, thus gaining a very clear knowledge of the various requirements of house planning for any section of the country.

One great trouble with Northern books and periodicals on architecture, is the lack of plans suited to Southern requirements. Enquiries like this are constantly coming in:

"Can you not get us up something suited to our peculiar wants?"

It is therefore the aim of this work to give designs suitable to any and all sections of the country, according to their various requirements.

There are many peculiar features in Southern house-planning that cannot be described, and can only be known by actual experience and long and careful study. With many of the designs in this book I have given plans for both North and South, but in this the true principles cannot be shown.

In all of my working drawings I have incorporated the principles required in any section of the country, and am not able to practically demonstrate it in any other way, as it is something that cannot be satisfactorily explained. How well I have carried out the foregoing principles in the work shown in this volume, I leave each reader to judge for himself.

HINTS

—TO—

Home-Builders.

THE plans and designs of cottages and houses presented in this volume have all been arranged with special care for *convenience* and *economy* of floor plans, with *pleasing exterior* design, the three things so eagerly sought by the intelligent and enterprising people of the day. To provide ample closet and cupboard room has been a leading thought in arranging each plan, knowing so well the great necessity and convenience of such rooms. When possible a bed room, with closet and bath room, has been arranged on the first floor, a bed room below being a great convenience in nearly every family.

There are many important features which ought to be included in the building of every house, but as they are not generally known by the parties intending to build, I have here given a few brief

HINTS TO HOME-BUILDERS.

A dry, well-kept cellar is healthier to live over than no cellar at all. Always drain your cellar with a good 4-inch to 6-inch tile, laying it around on the outside and a little below the wall, following the angles. This carries off the water before it can get into the cellar. With this tile should be connected all water from the eaves not wanted in the cistern. Traps should be used whenever necessary to prevent the inflow of gases.

Build all chimneys from the cellar bottom, and have ash pits. Dump all ashes below and clean out once a month or as often as necessary. The fire place will not draw unless the door opening in the ash pit in the cellar is kept closed tight. Use an iron door. It is not necessary to have an expensive mantel in order to have a good fire place.

Always try a chimney of any kind before the masons leave it, by burning paper or other matter in it to see that it draws well.

A smooth wall is necessary for a good job of papering. When two coats of brown mortar is used have last coat troweled down smooth, or go over it with a skim coat to smooth it up. Brown mortar left under as smooth floating as possible is best for painting upon. Painting can be done any time within two to three weeks after plastering is dry.

Always use double thick glass in all windows when other glass is not wanted, as single thick is too crooked for any use.

Never use oak for a kitchen floor, as it stains too easily by setting wet articles upon it. Ash is good; maple is best of all.

The outside dimensions of a house are taken in estimating siding, lath and plastering, stone and brick work. Corners of masonry are counted double, chimneys solid. Door and window openings are not counted out in estimating any of the above work, but in some localities it is customary to count out half the openings.

Brick veneered walls for outside purposes are cooler in summer, warmer in winter, forming dryer and stronger walls for ordinary buildings than any other class of materials I know of. It is a little more expensive than wood and cheaper than solid brick.

A slate roof at $8.00 per square—the price at which slate is figured in this work—costs about $3.00 per square more than shingled roofs.

Hardwood for interior finish costs about double that of paint work.

The gas piping of an ordinary cottage in this book costs from $5.00 to 8.00, and for the larger ones from $12.00 to $25.00. Gas light is cheapest and best when it can be had.

The expense of putting in a steam heater is about double that of a hot air furnace; their running expenses about equal.

The cost of erecting any of the houses given in this work in the South is from 5% to 8% less than the prices given.

Write to us concerning any changes wanted in plans, and keep writing till you get just what you want. Don't be afraid of writing too often. We are not easily offended.

Quite a number of fireplaces are shown in each floor plan in this work—only to give their location in case they are wanted—but to be omitted and their places supplied with sliding or other doorways, when they are not required.

INFORMATION CONCERNING OUR ESTIMATES, WORKING DRAWINGS, &C.

The estimates for the designs given in this book were made from the schedule of prices given on page, 167 and were prepared by Mr. W. C. Robinson, of Knoxville, Tenn., a native of Connecticut. He is a successful, practical contractor and builder of many years experience, and within the last eighteen months has erected from my plans the buildings shown on pages 14, 21, 82, 100, 118, 120, 122, (besides a number of others), to the entire satisfaction of the owner, the architect and himself. He is thus well prepared to judge of my drawings, and to know what and how to estimate to be as correct as it is possible to be. Under these circumstances I employed Mr. Robinson to give me a correct estimate on all the designs in this work, figured from scale drawings. The prices given for materials, &c., are intended to be an average for this country, and the estimates will be found to be right or full high for a majority of places; yet there are localities in which the estimates will be considered low; but a comparison of their local prices with our scheduled prices will show at what price any particular design can be executed. It is impossible in this work to give estimates to suit every individual want, each one being at liberty to include such extras as are most desirable.

Each design is figured to be a complete house outside of the following articles:

NOT INCLUDED IN THE ESTIMATES.

Owing to the wide diversity of styles and prices, the following articles were not included in our estimates, as a house can be completed without them:

Heating apparatus, range, hearth, mantels and grates; plumbing, other than that given in the description of each plan; draining or cementing of cellar; finished rooms in attic; papering of walls; plaster cornice or center pieces.

Aside from the above, each house is estimated to be completed ready for occupancy.

The following is

INCLUDED IN THE ESTIMATES.

For small cottages with brick foundations, 9-inch walls, and for larger houses 13-inch walls are estimated. Where stone is used a 12-inch wall for small and a 20-inch wall for the larger residences is used. In nearly every case the walls are for three feet high above grade line. Matched sheathing, with water-proof building paper under weatherboarding, is included in all estimates. Rafters to be boarded tight for slate and open for shingle roofs. Slate is counted in these estimates at $8.00 per square of 100 feet. Brick work for all chimneys; good hardburned brick is estimated for all work; large, heavy doors; double strength A. A. American sheet glass; good quality of hardware; galvanized iron gutters and conductors; porch floors 1¼-inch thick. Materials all of good quality and workmanship first-class throughout.

OUR WORKING DRAWINGS.

Knowing, as I do, that my working drawings, when they leave the office, go out of reach of my personal supervision, I have taken especial pains to make everything plain and easily understood by mechanics generally. Every detail that goes from the office is *full size* and drawn by hand (not printed.)

Everything requiring it has a detail given, and they are all ready to be pricked off on the material for working out.

Our prices given for complete working drawings are for blue print copies of the floor plans and elevations, and not for cloth tracings, the blue prints being just as good and exact reproductions of the original drawings. If on tracing cloth, $3.00 to $5.00 additional is charged.

WHAT A SET OF OUR WORKING PLANS CONSIST OF.

Basement or foundation plan, first and second floors, and where necessary, a roof plan. Elevations of front, right, left and rear views. All to a scale of one-quarter of an inch to the foot, with every dimension carefully figured and marked. Also a complete set of details, all full size. Printed blank specifications filled out as far as we can understand your requirements. Two blank contract forms and a sheet of color samples for outside painting, desscribing their application. Everything necessary for the builder is supplied.

In ordering plans, in which you would like slight changes, it is best to take the plans as they are and effect the change between yourself and builder, without additional cost. But if changes of importance are required it had better be left to us, for which our charges will always be moderate. Write for changes.

To the many who ask the question: "Do your buildings look as well when built as they show on paper?" I will say: It is the observation of every one who sees my buildings that they appear much better after being erected than they do on paper. And I can say, with confidence, to every reader, that there is not a design in this book but what will present a better and more beautiful appearance when built than they do in any of these engravings.

☞ *For schedule of prices of material and price-list of working plans,* **see pages 167 and 168.**

THE two scenes on the opposite page were engraved direct from photographs taken from real life in the Great Smoky Mountains of North Carolina in the vicinity of Asheville. The engravings are given for their oddity and picturesqueness. The contrast between these two homes and those on the following pages gives us an idea of the advancement of modern architecture in this country.

"UNCLE TOM'S CABIN."

"OLD CABIN HOME."

CONTRASTED ARCHITECTURE.

PERSPECTIVE VIEW.

Residence of H. H. KINCAID, Knoxville, Tenn.

DESIGN No. 1.

Cost to build, as per description, $5,250.

SIZE.

Over all except steps, 44x64 feet. First story, 11 feet; second story, 10 feet. Depth of cellar, 7 feet, under back part only.

OUTSIDE MATERIALS.

First and second stories weatherboarded, belts wainscoted and shingled, roof slated, foundation brick. Outside blinds. Painting, three-coat work.

This is a house of ample and convenient room, compact and well proportioned, of rather plain design, yet sensibly and tastefully finished. The hall is of ample size and is used as a sitting room. The parlor connects with hall by sliding doors and has a front window of plate and stained glass. The dining room is large and light and opens out on front veranda from the bay window. The sitting room is used as a family bed room, with a children's bed room back. The kitchen is conveniently arranged and is effectually cut off from front part of house by the back hall.

The chambers are ample in size and all are provided with closets. The round tower produces a very handsome effect, being in good proportion to the rest of the house.

We can recommend this design strongly for a first-class house. Variations of this plan can be seen on pages 80, 112, 122 and 166. This plan can be enlarged, reduced or changed to front in any direction.

(*See page 10.*)

FRONT VIEW. **DESIGN No. 1.**

INTERIOR

Parlor and hall are finished in antique oak; dining room in cherry or ash; sitting room, gum wood or butternut. Balance of rooms to be pine, with three coats of paint in desirable tints.

Plastering, three-coat work, hard finish.

Plumbing consists of sink and pump in kitchen, bath tub and bowl, with connections. Gas throughout.

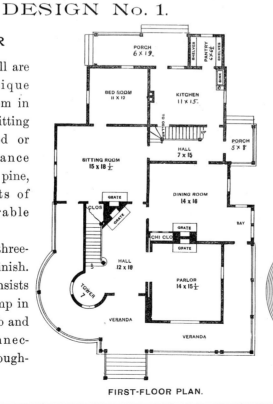

FIRST-FLOOR PLAN.

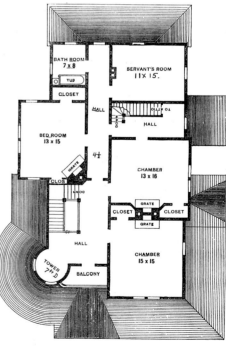

SECOND-FLOOR PLAN.

PERSPECTIVE VIEW. *Residence of T. W. FISK, Knoxville, Tenn.*

SIZE.

Over all, except steps, 36 feet 9 inches x 45 feet 9 inches.

Height of story, 10 feet; studding, 12 feet long; depth of cellar, 6 feet 6 inches under kitchen.

OUTSIDE MATERIALS.

The story is weatherboarded up to roof. Gables are wainscoted with a neat belt of ornamental cut shingles below. Roof, slated; foundation, brick. Painting, three-coat work. Outside blinds.

DESIGN No. 2.

Cost to build, as per description, $1,810.

NOTES.

The interior finish of this cottage is hardwoods for vestibule and parlor, and paint work for the rest.

The exterior appearance is ornate and very attractive, and as to the interior, the owner and all who see it are perfectly delighted with it. The vestibule, or hall, is large and opens into three principal rooms. The parlor and sitting rooms are connected by sliding doors and are admirably adapted for entertainments. The bath room opens into a bed room and a kitchen.

(*See page 10.*)

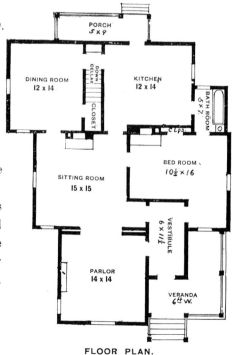

FLOOR PLAN.

PERSPECTIVE VIEW.

DESIGN No. 3.

Cost to build, as per description, $900 to $1,200.

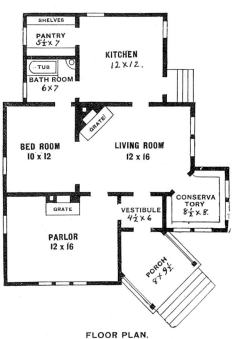

FLOOR PLAN.

OUTSIDE MATERIALS.

Body part weatherboarded, gables and roof shingled. Foundation brick. Painting, three-coat work. Outside blinds.

SIZE.

Over all except steps, 38x32 feet 6 inches. Height of story, 10 feet. Studding, 12 feet long. No cellar.

NOTES.

This is a one-story cottage, and has a nicely-arranged floor plan. The vestibule opens into the parlor and living room. The living room connects with the bed room by a large opening, which can be closed by folding doors or curtains. The kitchen is of good size and has a large, well-lighted pantry.

The conservatory, off from living room, is a very pretty feature in this plan, especially so when filled with blooming plants. If omitted, however, would save about $50 expense.

This plan can be changed in size or made to front in any direction desired.

(*See page 10.*)

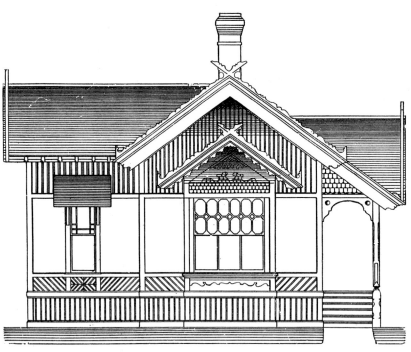

FRONT VIEW.

DESIGN No. 4.

Cost to build, as per description, **$500 to $700**.

OUTSIDE MATERIALS.

The main body is weatherboarded, gables and down to top of windows and lower belt wainscoted, roof shingled. Foundation posts and wainscoting all around. Painting, two-coat work.

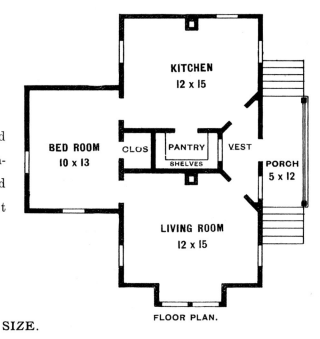

FLOOR PLAN.

SIZE.

Over all except steps, 31x31 feet 6 inches. Height of story, 10 feet. Studding, 12 feet long. No cellar.

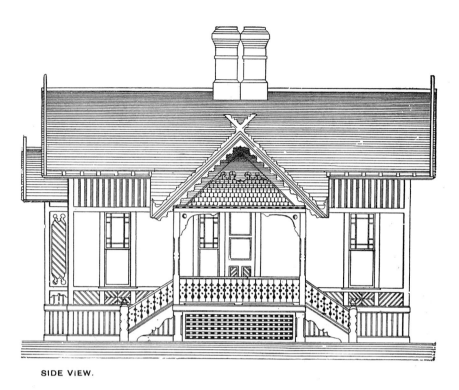

SIDE VIEW.

DESIGN No. 4.

NOTES.

We present herewith two elevations and a floor plan of a very neat little cottage, one designed to meet the requirements of a small family. The vestibule opens into the two principal rooms. The pantry is convenient and lighted by a window in the vestibule, the vestibule being lighted by a window and a glass door. A ventilator is built in ceiling of pantry. A large bed room opens from both the other rooms, has a large closet and is well lighted. This cottage is somewhat in the Swiss style. By leaving off bay window and making perfectly plain, this cottage could be erected for as little as $400 to $500.

It can be used as a summer cottage, servants' house or private residence for a small family.

The plan can be changed to suit any requirements.

(*See page 10.*)

PERSPECTIVE VIEW.

DESIGN No. 5.

Cost to build, as per description, **Plan No. 1**, $600 to $800; **No. 2**, $800 to $1,000.

SIZE.

Plan No. 1, 32x27 feet 6 inches : Plan No. 2, 32x40 feet.
Height of story, 10 feet. Length of studding, 12 feet. No cellar.

OUTSIDE MATERIALS.

Body of the house is weatherboarded, gables shingled, roof shingled. Foundation, brick. Three coats of paint. Outside blinds.

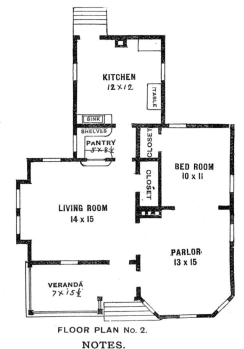

FLOOR PLAN No. 2.

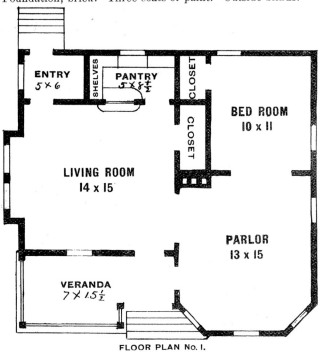

FLOOR PLAN No. I.

NOTES.

The interior is to be finished in pine or poplar, painted three coats. Plastering, three-coat work, hard finish. Plumbing includes sink and pump in kitchen, with connections. The two plans are the same, except that No. 2 shows a kitchen room added to rear.

We have in this a real tasty little cottage, with rooms of ample size and lots of good closets.

These plans can be changed in size or made to front in any direction.

(See page 10.)

SIZE.

Over all except steps, 24 feet 6 inches x 34 feet.

Height of story, 9 feet. Studding, 10 feet long. No cellar.

OUTSIDE MATERIALS.

Body weatherboarded, gables and roof shingled. Foundation, brick piers, with lattice work between. Painting, three-coat work. No blinds.

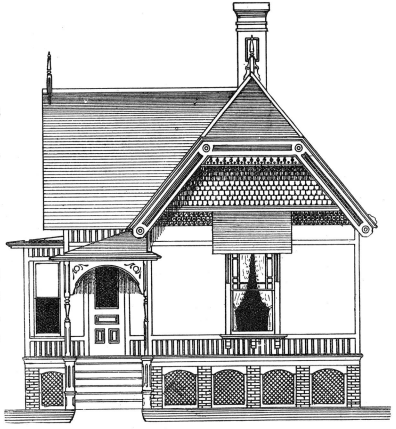

FRONT VIEW.

DESIGN No. 6.

Cost to build, as per description, $500.

NOTES.

This is a neat little inexpensive cottage, designed for erection in a village in Illinois. The foundation in this case is open, and would be too cold for winter, but by building the piers of brick, 12 inches square, the space between could be built up with a 4-inch wall of brick, making it cheap and warm. The hall opens into all the rooms. The kitchen has a nice large pantry, and the dining room, which is to be used as a living room, has a good closet, there is also a back hall and bath room. This, for a small cottage, is quite convenient and can be built upon a narrow lot.

The interior has a neat pine trim, painted two coats. Plaster, two coats, brown mortar.

The plan can be changed in size or made to front in any direction.

(*See page 10.*)

PANTRY
5 x 5½

HALL
4½'

BATH ROOM
5 x 6

KITCHEN
9 x 13

DINING ROOM
14 x 15

CLOSET

HALL
5½ x 13

PARLOR
12 x 15

PORCH
6 x 6

FLOOR PLAN.

LEFT SIDE VIEW.

DESIGN No. 7.

NOTES.

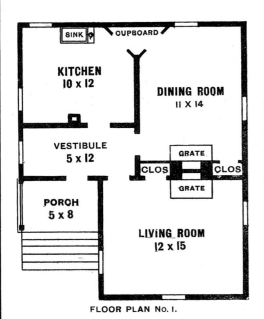

KITCHEN
10 x 12

DINING ROOM
11 X 14

VESTIBULE
5 x 12

GRATE
CLOS   CLOS
GRATE

PORCH
5 x 8

LIVING ROOM
12 x 15

FLOOR PLAN No. I.

Both views of this cottage are suited to Plan No. 1, which is intended for a one-story house, with windows in attic, access to which can be had by means of a step ladder through an opening in ceiling of vestibule or kitchen. This is a neat arrangement for a small house, the vestibule being large, well lighted and opening into all the rooms. A kitchen can be built on back at any future time if desired, making a good four-roomed house.

In Floor Plan No. 2 we have this same design carried up to a story and a half in height, the vestibule being made larger, in which stairs are placed.

All the rooms are made larger, a back hall and kitchen, with pantry and serving room, are added, and many other features are included, which will commend this plan to any one desiring a moderate-priced house.

This plan can be enlarged, reduced or changed to front in any direction.

(See page 10.)

FRONT VIEW.

INTERIOR.

Pine finish throughout. Painted three coats, neat tints. Plaster, two coats, brown mortar, trowel finish, for papering upon. Plumbing consists of sink and pump in kitchen, with connections for supply and waste water.

DESIGN No. 7.

Cost to build, as per description, Plan No. 1, $770; Plan No. 2, $1,400, raised to story and a half.

SIZE.

Plan No. 1, 24 feet 6 inches x 29 feet.

Height of story, 10 feet. Studding, 12 feet.

Plan No. 2, 33 feet 6 inches x 50 feet.

Height of first story, 9 feet; second story, 8 feet 6 inches. Studding, 14 feet. Small cellar, 6 feet 6 inches deep.

OUTSIDE MATERIALS.

First story, clapboarded; second story, shingled. Foundation walls of brick. Painting, three-coat work. Outside blinds all around.

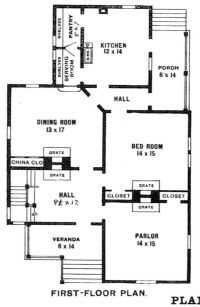

FIRST-FLOOR PLAN.

PLAN No. 2.

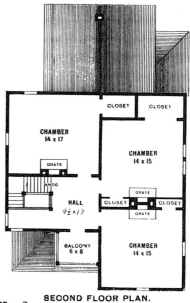

SECOND FLOOR PLAN.

PERSPECTIVE VIEW.

DESIGN No. 8.

Cost to build, as per description, Plan No. 1, $700; Plan No. 2, $1,000 to $1,200.

By omitting bay windows and all ornamental work in Plan No. 1 it could be built for from $400 to $500.

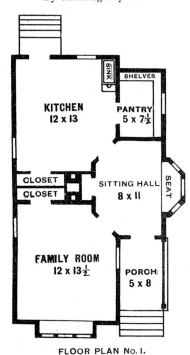

FLOOR PLAN No. I.

NOTES.

This is an artistic little home and contains a great deal of room, for the ground it occupies.

Plan No. 2 could be built upon a 25-foot lot, by omitting the bay window in sitting hall. This cottage can be built for almost any price from $400 up to $2,000, by making it plain or raising to a story and a half and adding a cellar.

The two floor plans are given to show how it may be changed and enlarged. Any one can get from these plans a cottage of convenience and beauty on a small scale. It would make a handsome seaside or summer cottage, or a tasty office building.

(*See page 10.*)

FRONT VIEW.

DESIGN No. 8.

SIZE.

Plan No. 1, 21x33 feet.

Plan No. 2, 26x47 feet.

Height of stories in each are 10 feet. Studding, 10 feet long. No cellar included.

OUTSIDE MATERIALS.

Main body weatherboarded, belts wainscoted, gables and roof shingled. Foundation of brick. Painting, three coats. Outside blinds.

FLOOR PLAN NO. 2.

INTERIOR.

The interior finish is of pine or poplar and to be painted three coats. The style of the trim is neat and in keeping with the exterior.

FRONT VIEW.

DESIGN No. 9.

Cost to build, as per description, **Plan No. 1, $985; Plan No. 2, $1,250.**

Both views are from plan No. 1.

SIZE.

Plan No. 1, 25 feet 6 inches x 33 feet.
Plan No. 2, 26 feet 6 inches x 48 feet.
Stories in each plan are 10 feet. Studding, 12 feet long. No cellar.

OUTSIDE MATERIALS.

Body of house is clapboarded, gables shingled and paneled, roof shingled. Foundation of brick. Outside blinds. Painting, three-coat work.

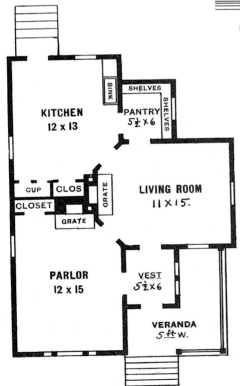

FLOOR PLAN NO. 1.

SIDE VIEW.

DESIGN No. 9.

NOTES.

This is a convenient and compact cottage, and in exterior appearance is as neat as any one could wish, for a house of its size and price. There are many conveniences, which can readily be seen by referring to the plans. By converting the pantry into a bath room this design would make a very handsome office for a corporation or private party desiring such a building. It is also well adapted for a summer or lakeside cottage. The roof in this design is one of its handsomest features

Plan No. 2 shows an enlargement of Plan No. 1 in size and number of rooms. From the back porch we enter the kitchen direct and the dining and living rooms through a small hall, which is provided with a closet for coats, &c.

These plans can be enlarged, reduced or changed to front in any direction.

(See page 10.)

FLOOR PLAN NO. 2.

PERSPECTIVE VIEW.

DESIGN No. 10.

Cost to build, as per description, $800 to $1,000.

SIZE.

Over all except steps, 26 feet 6 inches x 39 feet.
Height of story, 10 feet.   Studding, 12 feet long.   Depth of cellar, 6 feet 6 inches, under kitchen.

OUTSIDE MATERIALS.

Body weatherboarded, belts wainscoted, gables and roof shingled. Foundation, brick.   Painting, three coats.   Outside blinds.

NOTES.

This is another example of a one-story cottage. The attic is provided with windows for ventilation and light, in case that part is to be utilized for storing purposes. The kitchen is of good size and has a nice, large pantry. A cellar way can be arranged between pantry and closet if desired. The other rooms are conveniently arranged and of ample size for a house of this character. This cottage was recently erected at Aurora, Ill. The design is tasty, as all cottages should be. It costs nothing to get good proportions, and a few dollars expended in ornamental work adds to the value of the building many times the extra expense.

Any desired changes can be made in this plan.

(*See page 10.*)

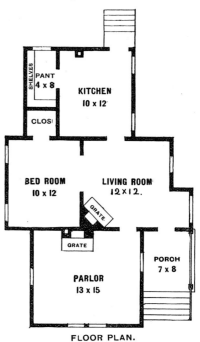

FLOOR PLAN.

FRONT VIEW.

DESIGN No. 11.

NOTES.

This cottage is fully described on page 30, it being the same house with smaller and reversed floor plans and slightly different in design.

This is intended for a tasty, inexpensive house, and can be used as a summer cottage if desired.

It can be changed to suit any requirements.

(*See page 10.*)

Cost to build, as per description, $1,400.

SIZE.

Over all except steps, 26 feet 6 inches x 36 feet.

Height of first story, 9 feet; second story, 8 feet 4 inches.

Depth of cellar, 6 feet 6 inches, under all.

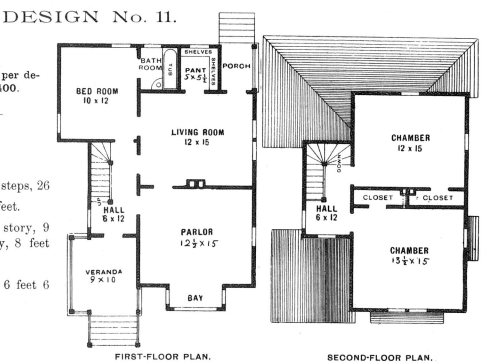

FIRST-FLOOR PLAN.   SECOND-FLOOR PLAN.

PERSPECTIVE VIEW.

DESIGN No. 12.

Cost to build, as per description, $1,476.

NOTES.

—

The illustrations here given are for a plain yet neat and tasty cottage, with four rooms below and two above. There is a neat entrance hall, which opens into the three principal rooms. The kitchen is of good size and opens into family room, dining room, pantry and out on to back porch. The family room is of good size and can be connected with parlor by removing fire places and substituting sliding or folding doors.

The second story speaks for itself. The room marked balcony is a closet instead, and could be used as a small bath room if desired. The two bay windows could be omitted with a saving of about $30 each.

This plan can be enlarged, reduced or changed to front in any direction.

(*See page 10.*)

FRONT VIEW.

DESIGN No. 28.

SIZE.

Plan No. 1, 27 feet x 46 feet. Height of first story, 9 feet; second story, 9 feet.

Plan No. 2, 27 feet x 39 feet 6 inches. Height of first story, 10 feet; second story, 9 feet 4 inches.

Depth of cellar, 6 feet 6 inches, under one-half of house.

OUTSIDE MATERIALS.

First story is weatherboarded. Second story, belts and gables are half timbered and shingled. Roof slated. Stone foundation. Painting, three-coat work. Outside blinds throughout.

NOTES.

The disposition of the veranda and balcony and the parlor bay window renders this a very attractive front. The rooms, though small, are conveniently arranged.

Floor Plan No. 2, from which the views were made, is a high story and a half house; but plan No. 1 is for two full stories. Hence there is quite a difference in the price of the two. Either one of them can be made to cost less money, as you will see by referring to the materials used in the estimates.

These plans can be enlarged, reduced or changed to front in any direction.

(*See page 10.*)

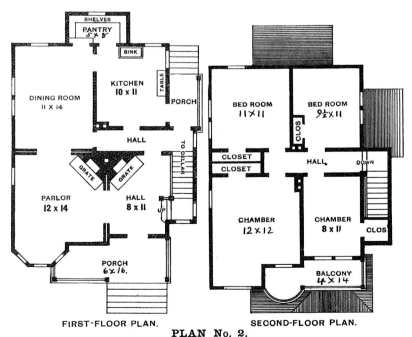

FIRST-FLOOR PLAN. **SECOND-FLOOR PLAN.**

PLAN No. 2.

PERSPECTIVE VIEW.   *BRICK RESIDENCE.*

DESIGN No. 29.

Cost to build, as per description, $4,440.

NOTES.

There is not enough ornamental work on this building to make it expensive, only enough to make a tasty and attractive front, the intention being to produce a neat but substantial brick cottage for a narrow lot. By using cheaper material and making perfectly plain the house could be built for about $3,500.

The hall is entered from a vestibule, the two being separated by an arch and curtains. The hall extends back to kitchen and pantry, by which means the front part of the house is cut off from the cooking apartments. The dining room contains an excellent china closet and also opens on to back porch. The cellar way is under the stairs, convenient to the kitchen. A back stair has not been considered necessary, owing to the privacy of the front stairs.

The second story contains a servant's room, a good bath room, two elegant chambers, with large closets and dressing room.

This house could be erected in wood for about $2,500.

The plans can be enlarged, reduced or changed to front in any direction.

(*See page 10.*)

FRONT VIEW.

INTERIOR.

Parlor is to be finished in oak; balance of house painted three coats. Plastering, three coats, hard finish. Plumbing consists of sink and pump in kitchen, bath tub and bowl, with connections, gas throughout.

DESIGN No. 29.

SIZE.

Over all except steps, 23 feet 6 inches x 56 feet.

Height of first story, 9 feet; second story, 8 feet 4 inches.

Depth of cellar, 6 feet 6 inches, under all except parlor.

OUTSIDE MATERIALS.

Walls and gables of brick (13-inch walls). Foundation, stone. Roof slated. Outside blinds.

FIRST-FLOOR PLAN.

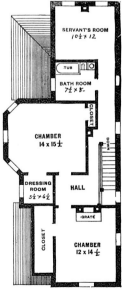

SECOND-FLOOR PLAN.

PERSPECTIVE VIEW.

DESIGN No. 30.

Cost to build, as per description, $3,450.

NOTES.

This house is well suited for a small family in any locality, and is also a handsome design for a seaside or summer cottage.

The veranda is neat and extends around the entire front. Dignity and expression is imparted to the entire structure by a handsome and well-proportioned square tower arising above the vestibule entrance on the left side. A neat arch, draped with tasty curtains, separates the dining room from alcove, which can be used as a small conservatory. The rear hall is a great convenience, opening as it does into three principal rooms.

This plan can be enlarged, reduced or changed to front in any direction.

(*See page 10.*)

FRONT VIEW.

INTERIOR.

Parlor and hall finished in natural oak, dining room ash or cherry, balance of house to have three coats of paint. Plastering, three-coat work, hard finish. Plumbing consists of sink and pump in kitchen, bath tub and bowl, with connections to all, gas throughout.

DESIGN No. 30

SIZE.

Over all except steps, 31 feet x 52 feet.

Height of first story, 10 feet; second story, 9 feet 4 inches.

Depth of cellar, 7 feet, under kitchen, hall and dining room.

OUTSIDE MATERIALS.

First and second stories weatherboarded, belts wainscoted, gables shingled and wainscoted, roof slated. Foundation of stone. Three coats painting. Outside blinds throughout.

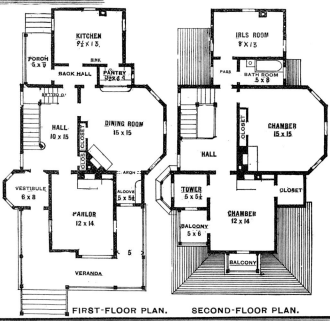

FIRST-FLOOR PLAN.   SECOND-FLOOR PLAN.

PERSPECTIVE VIEW.

DESIGN No. 31.

Cost to build, as per description, $2,860.

NOTES.

This house has a limited amount of hall space, but opens conveniently into the three principal rooms, all of which are of good size. The bath room is convenient to the family or sitting room and also to the kitchen, from which warm water can be supplied when other water supplies are not put in.

The second story is of very much the same plan as the first. The treatment of porch and balcony is novel and works out handsomely. A more elaborate treatment of this same design, with few changes, is shown on page 115. The porch and balcony in the two designs are identical.

This plan can be enlarged, reduced or changed to front in any direction.

(*See page 10.*)

FRONT VIEW.

INTERIOR.

The hall, parlor and sitting room are trimmed in any desirable hardwoods, natural finish. Balance of rooms are to be painted three coats. Plastering, three coat work, hard finish. Plumbing consists of sink and pump in kitchen, bath tub and bowl, with connections, gas throughout.

DESIGN No. 31.

SIZE.

Over all except steps, 32 feet 6 inches x 50 feet 6 inches.

Height of first story, 10 feet; second story, 9 feet 4 inches.

Depth of cellar, 6 feet 6 inches, under kitchen and pantry.

OUTSIDE MATERIALS.

First and second stories clapboarded, center belt and gables shingled, roof shingled. Foundation of brick. Painting three-coat work. Outside blinds throughout.

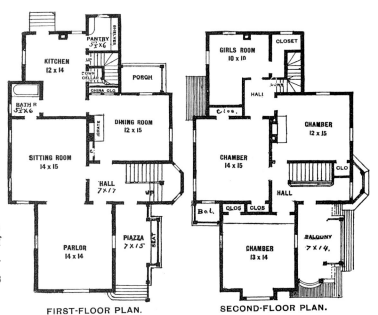

FIRST-FLOOR PLAN.   **SECOND-FLOOR PLAN.**

PERSPECTIVE VIEW.

DESIGN No. 32.

Cost to build, as per description, $2,700.

NOTES.

The vestibule can be made very attractive by carrying a neat arch across over stair newel from corner of parlor.

The arrangement of the stairway in the hall presents a beautiful appearance from the dining room. The stained glass in the windows enclosing the staircase extend from the stairs to the top of the bay, far above the second floor, presenting an appearance that must be seen to get the rich effect it produces. The glass is leaded cathedral, to cost $1.50 per foot.

This plan can be enlarged, reduced or changed to front in any direction.

(*See page 10.*)

INTERIOR.

Parlor, hall and dining room finished in oak; the balance of the house in white pine or poplar, to be painted three coats, smoothed down to a handsome finish. Plastering, three-coat work, hard finish. Plumbing consists of sink and pump in kitchen, bath tub and bowl, with connections, gas throughout.

The back hall is a very convenient feature of this plan, cutting the kitchen off, as it does, from the main part of the house and yet being perfectly convenient.

The dining-room bay is floored up level with the window sill, making a convenient seat or a handsome place for plants.

This plan will bear careful study.

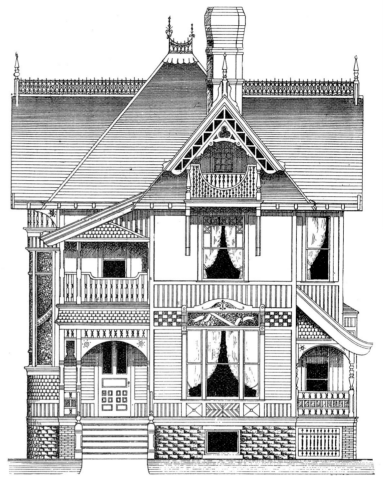

FRONT VIEW.

DESIGN No. 32.

SIZE.

Over all except steps, 31 feet 6 inches x 47 feet 6 inches.

Height of first story, 10 feet; second story, 9 feet 4 inches.

Depth of cellar, 6 feet 6 inches, under all.

OUTSIDE MATERIALS.

First and second stories clapboarded, belts wainscoted, gables shingled, roof slated. Slating alone, nailed on, estimated at $8 per square. Painting, three-coat work. Outside blinds throughout. Foundation walls of stone.

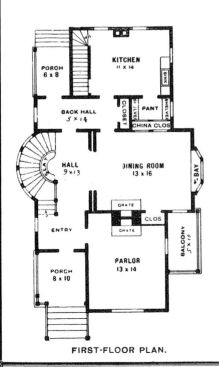

FIRST-FLOOR PLAN.

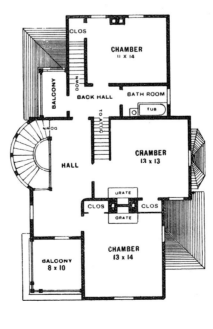

SECOND-FLOOR PLAN.

PERSPECTIVE VIEW.   *Residence of CHAS. J. BURTON, Gloversville, N. Y.*

DESIGN No. 33.

FIRST-FLOOR PLAN.   **PLAN No. 1.**   **SECOND-FLOOR PLAN.**

Cost to build, as per description, Plan **No. 1**, $3,000; Plan **No. 2**, $3,850.

INTERIOR.

Hall, parlor, sitting room and dining room are to be finished in hardwoods; balance three coats of paint, all first-class work. Plastering, three-coat work, hard finish. Plumbing consists of sink and pump in kitchen, bath tub and bowl, with connections, and gas throughout.

NOTES.

Architecturally this house is considered attractive and well proportioned. The horseshoe window in second story bay is tasty and becoming. The plan is convenient and speaks for itself. This house has recently been erected with the first story veneered with brick, second story and roof slated. It is very substantial and handsome. Those who desire such a house can have it in the same treatment, or brick all the way up, either veneered or solid walls.

This plan can be enlarged, reduced or changed to front in any direction.

(See page 10.)

FRONT VIEW.

DESIGN No. 33.

SIZE.

Over all except steps, 31x56 feet.
Height of first story, 10 feet; second story, 9 feet 4 inches.
Depth of cellar, 6 feet 6 inches, under all except hall and parlor.

OUTSIDE MATERIALS.

If in wood, the stories are both clapboarded, belt shingled and wainscoted, roof shingled. Foundation of stone.

FIRST-FLOOR PLAN.   PLAN No. 2.   SECOND-FLOOR PLAN.

First-floor plan labels: SINK, SHELVES, PANT 5 x 7, SHELVES, KITCHEN 9 x 12, SHELVES, CLOSET, PORCH, GRATE, BACK HALL, DINING ROOM 13 x 14, SITTING ROOM 14 x 14, GRATE, CLOS, GRATE, HALL 8 x 16, PARLOR 13 x 16, PIAZZA 8 x 12

Second-floor plan labels: CLOS, SERVANT'S ROOM 9 x 12, CLOSET, CHAMBER 14 x 14, CHAMBER 14 x 15, BATH ROOM, GRATE, TUB, CLOSET, GRATE, HALL, CHAMBER 14 x 18, TOWER, BALCONY 8 x 9

PERSPECTIVE VIEW.

DESIGN No. 34.

Cost to build, as per description, $3,000.

NOTES.

—

Very little space is taken up by the hall, yet it gives access to all the rooms on first floor. The hall closet and the stairs leading from the hall and kitchen, with cellar way underneath, are features of economy of space and very convenient. On the first floor a small music room is provided, and a neat curtain should drape the broad doorway between it and the parlor. A curtain is also drawn across the dining-room nook, which is a cosy retreat. The windows to porch on the right open to floor. The parlor bay window has a rich treatment of plate and stained glass. The dressing room, off from the front chamber, is a very desirable feature.

This plan can be enlarged, reduced or changed to front in any direction.

(*See page 10.*)

FRONT VIEW.

INTERIOR.

Music room and parlor are finished in oak; balance of house in pine or poplar, for painting three-coat work, tinted to suit. Plastering, three-coat work, hard finish. Plumbing consists of sink and pump in kitchen, bath tub and bowl, all with connections, and gas throughout.

OUTSIDE MATERIALS.

First and second stories clapboarded, belts shingled and wainscoted, roof shingled. Foundation of stone. Outside blinds. Painting, three-coat work.

DESIGN No. 34.

SIZE.

Over all except steps, 32x41 feet.

Height of first story, 10 feet; second story, 9 feet 4 inches.

Depth of cellar, 6 feet 6 inches, under kitchen, hall and pantry.

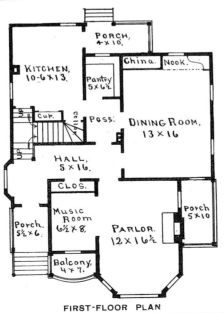

FIRST-FLOOR PLAN

KITCHEN, 10-6 X 13.
PORCH, 4 X 10.
China. Nook.
Pantry 5 X 6½
Cup.
cellar
Pass.
DINING ROOM. 13 X 16
HALL, 5 X 16.
CLOS.
Porch. 5½ X 6.
MUSIC ROOM 6½ X 8
PARLOR. 12 X 16½
Porch 5 X 10
Balcony, 4 X 7.

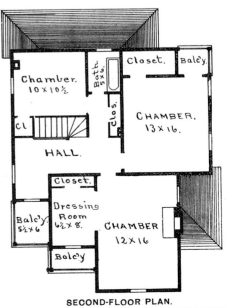

SECOND-FLOOR PLAN.

Chamber. 10 X 10½
Bath 5 X 6.
Closet. Balc'y.
Cl
Clos.
CHAMBER, 13 X 16.
HALL.
Closet.
Balc'y 5½ X 6
Dressing Room 6½ X 8.
CHAMBER 12 X 16
Balc'y

PERSPECTIVE VIEW.   *Residence of W. O. HAWORTH, Knoxville, Tenn.*

DESIGN No. 35.

Cost to build, as per description, $3,350.

NOTES.

This cottage was first erected for Mr. W. O. Haworth, at Knoxville, Tenn., and is very much admired for its proportions and handsome appearance. The front veranda is spacious and forms an important feature of the design. The balcony above is also very prominent and attractive. The hall is novelly arranged and contains a tasty but inexpensive staircase. The kitchen, pantry, back stairs, cellar way, rear hall and bath room are very conveniently grouped. The odors of cooking are cut off from front part of house.

This plan can be enlarged, reduced or changed to front in any direction.

(*See page 10.*)

FRONT VIEW.

DESIGN No. 35.

INTERIOR.

The hall, parlor, dining room and bed rooms are to be finished in oak or other hardwoods, natural wood finish. All the rest is for paint work, three coats. Plastering, three-coat work, hard finish. Plumbing consists of sink and pump in kitchen, bath tub and bowl, all with supply and waste pipe connections, gas throughout.

SIZE.

Over all except steps, 34 feet x 57 feet. Height of first story, 10 feet; second story, 9 feet 4 inches.

Depth of cellar, 7 feet, under kitchen and rear hall.

OUTSIDE MATERIALS.

First and second stories are weatherboarded, belts wainscoted, gables shingled, roof slated. Foundation, brick. Outside blinds. Painting, three-coat work.

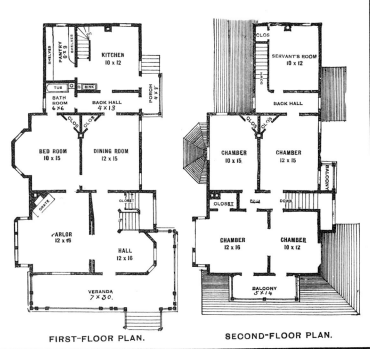

FIRST-FLOOR PLAN.   **SECOND-FLOOR PLAN.**

PERSPECTIVE VIEW.

DESIGN No. 36.

Cost to build, as per description, $3,180.

NOTES.

—

This design has been arranged with a view of filling a universal demand for a house of this character. The exterior is all that any one could desire, the veranda especially forming a very important part in bringing out the true proportions of the structure.

Through the vestibule, from the front, we enter the hall, which is large and handsomely arranged. The staircase is intended to be beautiful in plan and design. A front view from the hall is obtained from the nook which is cut off from hall by a neat arch. The fireplace, with a nice mantel, adds very much to the trimmings and embellishments of the hall.

The parlor and dining room are connected by sliding doors. The bed room has been made narrow in order to get a good closet and a large bath room. A good change, however, would be to make this room into a dining room and the dining room into a sitting room, omitting the closet in the bed room and shortening the bath room into a serving room and connecting with the kitchen. The back hall, while serving as a rear entrance, cuts the kitchen off from main part of house, thus preventing the odors of cooking from entering the living apartments.

In the second story there are four good rooms. The hall occupies very little space, only serving as an entrance way to all the rooms. It connects with the back hall, where the back and attic stairs are reached. Chimneys are arranged so that stoves may be used for heating, but furnace or steam heat is preferable.

This plan can be enlarged, reduced or changed to front in any direction.

(*See page 10.*)

FRONT VIEW.

INTERIOR.

The hall, parlor, dining and bed rooms are finished in oak or other desirable hardwood; all the rest is finished in pine or poplar, for painting. Plastering, three-coat work, hard finish. Plumbing consists of sink and pump in kitchen, bath tub and bowl, with supply and waste pipe connections, and gas throughout.

DESIGN No. 36.

SIZE.

Over all except steps, 31 feet 6 inches x 57 feet.

Height of first story, 10 feet; second story, 9 feet 4 inches.

Depth of cellar, 7 feet, under all.

OUTSIDE MATERIALS.

The entire building, up to cornice, is weatherboarded; gables and roof shingled. Foundation of stone. Outside blinds. Painting, three-coat work.

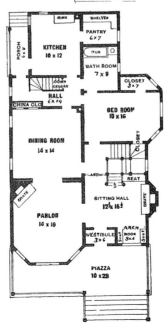

FIRST-FLOOR PLAN.

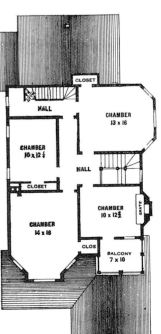

SECOND-FLOOR PLAN

PERSPECTIVE VIEW.   *Residence of C. D. DRAIN, Drain, Oregon.*

DESIGN No. 37.

Cost to build, as per description, $4,535.

NOTES.

In this design the main living and dining room has been given prominence, being large and provided with a nice bay window, thus affording a good view to the front. There is also connected with this room a large closet, with shelves and drawers, which will be found a great convenience. It will be observed that the kitchen, pantry, back stairs, cellar way, bath room and bed room on first floor are all conveniently arranged. The front entrance is unique, and a neat stairway is provided in hall. The tower is round above first story and is a very attractive feature. The second-floor arrangement is not less convenient than the first.

This plan can be enlarged, reduced or changed to front in any direction.

(*See page 10.*)

FRONT VIEW.

DESIGN No. 37.

INTERIOR.

Parlor and hall finished in natural oak; living room, cherry or sycamore; bed room, butternut or ash; balance of house painted three-coat work. Plastering, three-coat work, hard finish. Plumbing consists of sink and pump in kitchen, bath tub and bowl, with connections for all, and gas throughout.

SIZE.

Over all, except steps, 39 feet x 54 feet.

Height of first story, 10 feet; second story, 9 feet 4 inches. Depth of cellar, under all, 7 feet.

OUTSIDE MATERIALS.

Siding or weatherboarding is used on first and second stories, shingles on gables and center belt, beaded wainscoting on lower belt. Slate roof. Stone foundation. Outside blinds throughout. Painting, three coats.

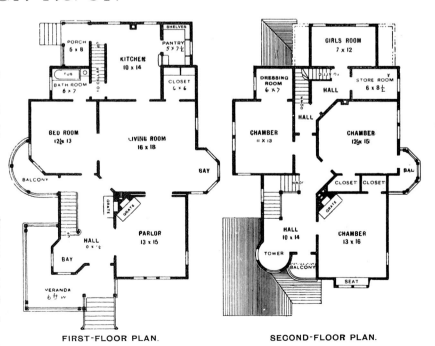

FIRST-FLOOR PLAN.   SECOND-FLOOR PLAN.

PERSPECTIVE VIEW.

DESIGN No. 38.

Cost to build, as per description,
Plan No. 1, $2,550;
No. 2, $2,760.

SIZE.

Plan No. 1, 31 feet x 44 feet.
Plan No. 2, 36 feet x 53 feet.
Height of first stories, 10 feet;
second stories, 9 feet 4 inches.
Depth of cellar, 6 feet 6 inches,
under all except parlor and hall.

OUTSIDE MATERIALS.

Both stories and center belt
weatherboarded, gables and roof
shingled. Foundation of brick.
Outside blinds. Painting, three-
coat work.

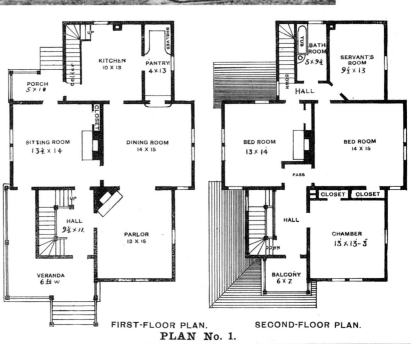

FIRST-FLOOR PLAN.   SECOND-FLOOR PLAN.

PLAN No. 1.

FRONT VIEW.

This is a house that has proven a universal favorite, and has been duplicated several times. Owing to the location of this house, we failed to get a good photograph, and in consequence the engraving shown does not do the house justice. It is a much better looking house than is here shown. The kitchen, pantry and dining room connections will be found to be very convenient.

This plan can be enlarged, reduced or changed to face in any direction.

(*See page 10.*)

DESIGN No. 38.

INTERIOR.

Three rooms and front hall on first floor to be in hardwood, natural finish. Balance of house finished for painting, three-coat work. Plastering, three-coat work, hard finish. Plumbing consists of sink and pump in kitchen, bath tub and bowl, with connections, and gas throughout.

FIRST-FLOOR PLAN.　　　SECOND-FLOOR PLAN.

PLAN No. 2.

PERSPECTIVE VIEW.   *Residence of GEO. R. WRIGHT, Knoxville, Tenn.*

DESIGN No. 39.

Cost to build, as per description, Plan No. 1, $2,950; Plan No. 2. $3,400

SIZE.

Plan No. 1, 32 feet 6 inches x 44 feet.

Plan No. 2, 33 feet x 57 feet.

Height of first story, 10 feet; second story, 9 feet 4 inches.

Depth of cellar, 7 feet, under all except parlor and hall.

OUTSIDE MATERIALS.

First and second stories clapboarded, center belt and gables shingled, roof slated, foundation brick. Painting, three-coat work. Outside blinds throughout.

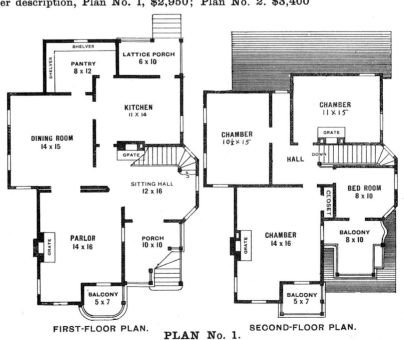

FIRST-FLOOR PLAN.   SECOND-FLOOR PLAN.

PLAN No. 1.

FRONT VIEW. **DESIGN No. 39.**

NOTES.

This is an attractive front for a suburban residence, being well broken in outline and of handsome and novel design; the proportions being all that can be desired. The main roof sweeps down over the porch, in which the steps ascend in a wind, the corner of the roof resting on the newel post of the steps. The balcony, constructed within this roof and under the projecting gable, is very roomy and pleasant. The sitting hall is very convenient and is provided with a neat mantel and grate under the stairs. The stairs are of neat design but not expensive.

This house looks equally well with or without the kitchen extension shown in Floor Plan No. 2.

We call your attention to this as a first-class house of its size, its general appearance being very striking.

This plan can be enlarged, reduced or changed to front in any direction.

(See page 10.)

INTERIOR.

Parlor and hall are finished in oak. All the other rooms are to be painted three coats, on pine or poplar finish. Plastering, three-coat work, hard finish. Plumbing consists of sink and pump in kitchen, bath tub and bowl, with connections, and gas throughout.

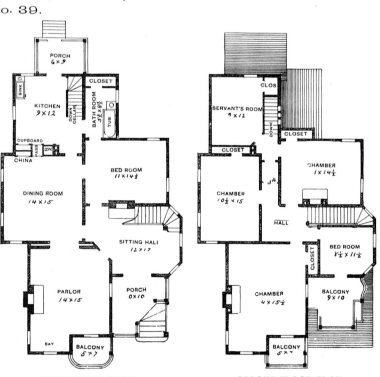

FIRST-FLOOR PLAN. **PLAN No. 2.** **SECOND-FLOOR PLAN.**

PERSPECTIVE VIEW.   *Residence of F. E. McARTHUR, Knoxville, Tenn.*

DESIGN No. 40.

Cost to build, as per description, $2,975.

NOTES.

It will be observed that instead of having a hall on first floor we have a rather large vestibule entrance, which opens into the two principal rooms. The dining room is separated from the parlor by curtains and the bed room by sliding doors. The stairway is accessible from the dining and bed rooms and is an easy flight. The kitchen is cut off from the dining room by a well-fitted serving room. There is also a large store room or pantry off from kitchen. The porches are ample and the bay window in parlor is glazed with handsome glass. The second story will be found ample and convenient. The hall is well lighted by transoms over the doors.

This is a very attractive design, and has been erected several times.

This plan can be enlarged, reduced or changed to front in any direction.

(See page 10.)

FRONT VIEW.

INTERIOR.

The vestibule, parlor, dining room and bed room are finished in hardwoods. Balance of house is painted work. Plastering, three-coat work, hard finish. Plumbing consists of sink and pump in kitchen, bath tub and bowls, with connections.

DESIGN No. 40.

SIZE.

Over all, except steps, 33 feet 6 inches x 46 feet 6 inches. Height of first story, 10 feet; second story, 9 feet 4 inches. Depth of cellar, 7 feet under all.

OUTSIDE MATERIALS.

First and second stories clapboarded, belts wainscoted, roof slated. Foundation, stone. Painting, three-coat work. Outside blinds throughout.

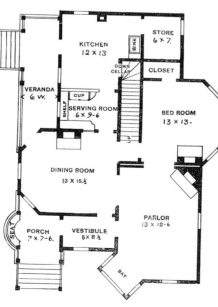

FIRST-FLOOR PLAN.

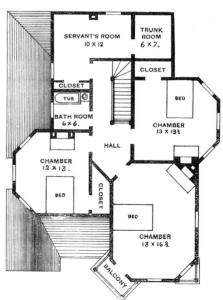

SECOND-FLOOR PLAN.

SIZE.

Plan No. 1, 38x59 feet.

Plan No. 2, 36x56 feet.

Height of stories in both plans—First story, 10 feet; second story, 9 feet 4 inches. Depth of cellar, 7 feet under all.

PERSPECTIVE VIEW.

Residence of CHAS. E. BRADT, De Kalb, Ill.

DESIGN No. 41.

Cost to build, as per description, Plan No. 1, $4,000; Plan No. 2, $3,800.

OUTSIDE MATERIALS.

First and second stories clapboarded, belts wainscoted, gables and roof shingled. Stone foundation. Painting, three-coat work. Outside blinds throughout.

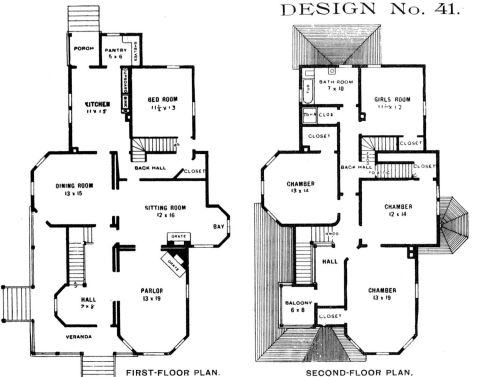

FIRST-FLOOR PLAN.

SECOND-FLOOR PLAN.

PLAN No. 1.

FRONT VIEW.

DESIGN No. 41.

NOTES.

This house was first erected from my plans in 1888, and since then has been erected over one hundred times in the United States and Canada, on nearly as many different floor-plan arrangements, and at prices ranging from $3,000 to $8,500. In this work we give two sets of floor plans, one as usually adopted in a Northern climate and one giving a general arrangement for Southern requirements. This house was erected for Mr. Wm. Weiss, of Beaumont, Texas, at a cost of over $8,500. A photographic reproduction of his hall will be found on page 121.

It will be seen that the rooms are of good size, well connected and convenient. The front parlor window and the one in side of sitting room bay window are of plate glass, with stained glass transoms. The kitchen is large, having good pantry and cupboard room. Each plan has a bed room on first floor, which is provided with closets and is convenient to back stairs.

These plans can be enlarged, reduced or changed to front in any direction.

(See page 10.)

INTERIOR.

Hall, parlor, dining and sitting rooms are finished in hard woods. Balance of rooms are pine or poplar, for paint work. Plastering is three-coat work, hard finish. Plumbing consists of sink and pump in kitchen, bath tub and bowl, with connections, gas throughout.

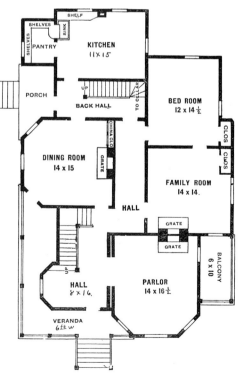

FIRST-FLOOR PLAN.

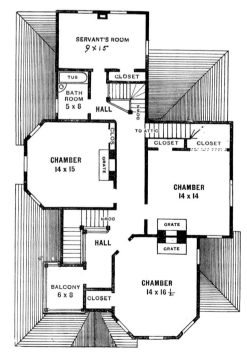

SECOND-FLOOR PLAN.

PLAN No. 2.

PERSPECTIVE VIEW.

DESIGN No. 42.

Cost to build, as per description, Plan No. 1, $3,625; Plan No. 2, $4,550.

SIZE.

Plan No. 1, 39x47 feet.
Plan No. 2, 40x59 feet.
Height of first story, 10 feet 6 inches; second story, 10 feet. Depth of cellar, 7 feet, under all, both plans.

OUTSIDE MATERIALS.

First and second stories weatherboarded, belts wainscoted, roof slated. Foundation, stone. Painting, three-coat work. Outside blinds.

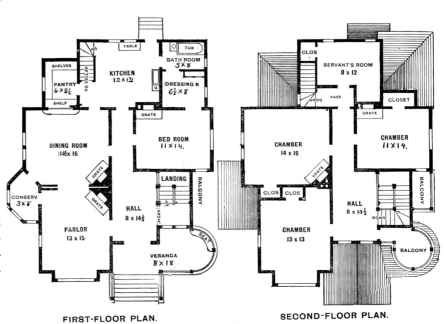

FIRST-FLOOR PLAN.

SECOND-FLOOR PLAN.

PLAN No. 1.

We present this house with the belief that it will be appreciated for its general proportions, style and convenient arrangement of floor plans. The veranda, with its dome-roofed balcony, is spacious and attractive, the gable roof extending over the steps, as in several other designs. The hall is a beautiful feature, having the stairway separated from the main room by a handsome arched screen. All the main rooms are reached from the hall, and closets are provided wherever necessary.

The accommodations and conveniences of the kitchen and its surroundings can be seen by a glance at the floor plans.

The second floor is arranged with special regard to convenience, ample closet and store room being provided. A stairway leads from the back hall to a large and well-lighted attic, which can be finished off into rooms for any purpose.

These plans can be enlarged, reduced or changed to front in any direction.

(See page 10.)

FRONT VIEW.

DESIGN No. 42.

INTERIOR.

Hall, parlor and dining room finished in oak; balance of rooms paint work. Plastering, three-coat work, hard finish. Plumbing consists of sink and pump in kitchen, bath tub and bowl with connections; gas throughout.

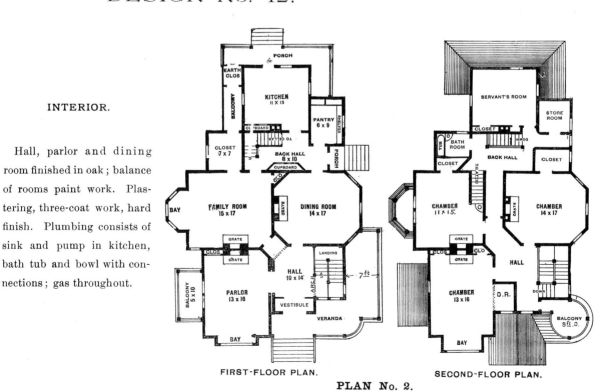

FIRST-FLOOR PLAN.

SECOND-FLOOR PLAN.

PLAN No. 2.

INTERIOR.

All rooms on first floor, except kitchen, are to be finished in hard pine; balance of rooms painted three coats. Plastering, three-coat work, hard finish. Plumbing consists of pump and sink in kitchen, bath tub and bowl, with connections, gas throughout.

PERSPECTIVE VIEW.   *Residence of WAYNE L. HAWORTH, Knoxville, Tenn.*

DESIGN No. 43.

Cost to build, as per description, Plan No. 1, $3,600; Plan No. 2, $3,000.

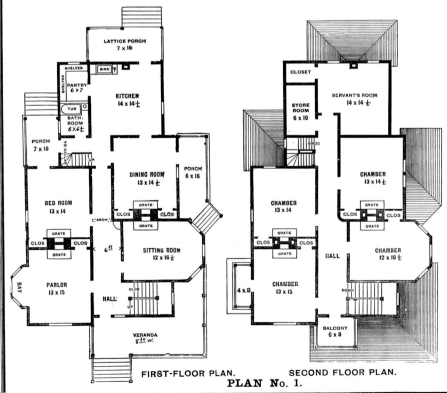

FIRST-FLOOR PLAN.   SECOND FLOOR PLAN.

PLAN No. 1.

NOTES.

No. 1 shows the plans and perspective view of a residence recently erected for Mr. Wayne L. Haworth, at Knoxville, Tenn., and has an arrangement of rooms such as is usually required in a warm climate. The veranda is of good size and the rooms, if not ample, can be enlarged to any size. The main hall connects with back hall, which opens into dining room, kitchen, bath room, back stairs, cellar way and out on to back porch. The kitchen, which is of good size, has a large and well-lighted pantry. In a climate where fireplaces are not used for heating purposes a nice effect can be produced by connecting the two principal rooms on either side of the hall by sliding doors in place of the grates.

PERSPECTIVE VIEW.

Residence of J. E. HATCH, Garrettsville, Ohio.

NOTES.

In plan No. 2 we have the residence of Mr. J. E. Hatch, of Garrettsville, Ohio. It is a design that works up admirably in the building, presenting a much more tasty appearance than the illustration shows.

The rooms are of ample size and convenient. There are front and back stairs. The bath room is on the first floor and is reached from the bed room through a large closet.

The second story is convenient, each room being provided with ample closets. A hall extends through the house, connecting the front and back stairs and giving access to all the rooms. A narrow stairway leads to the attic. A tank is located in the rear of house, over the bath room.

(*See page 10.*)

DESIGN No. 43.

SIZE.

Over all except steps—Plan No. 1, 41x66 feet; Plan No. 2, 34x46 feet. Height of first story—Plan No. 1, 10 feet 6 inches; second story, 9 feet 6 inches. Height of first story—Plan No. 2, 10 feet; second story, 9 feet 4 inches, Depth of cellar, 7 feet under all.

OUTSIDE MATE-RIALS.

First and second stories clapboarded, belts wainscoted, gables and roof shingled. Foundation of brick. Outside blinds. Painting, three-coat work.

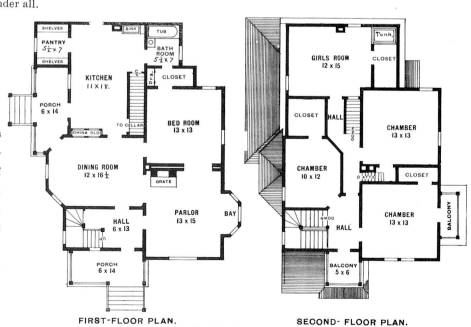

FIRST-FLOOR PLAN.

SECOND-FLOOR PLAN.

PLAN No. 2.

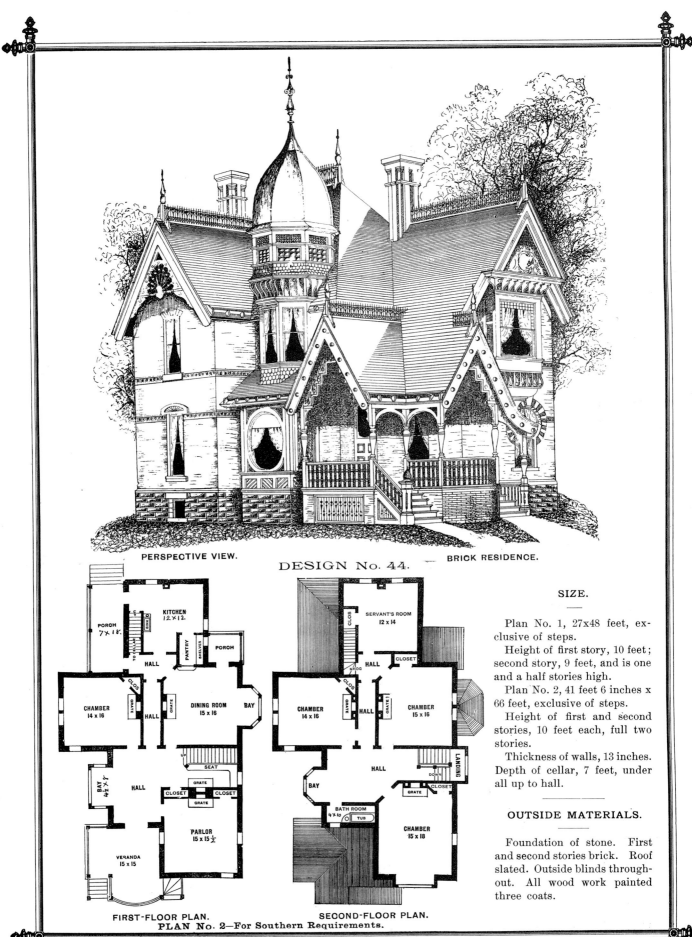

PERSPECTIVE VIEW.   DESIGN No. 44.   BRICK RESIDENCE.

FIRST-FLOOR PLAN.

KITCHEN
12 x 12

PORCH
7 x 18.

TO CELLAR

HALL

PANTRY

SHELVES

PORCH

CHAMBER
14 x 16

CLOS

GRATE

HALL

GRATE

DINING ROOM
15 x 16

BAY

UP

SEAT

BAY
4½ x 5

HALL

CLOSET

GRATE

CLOSET

GRATE

PARLOR
15 x 15½

VERANDA
15 x 15

SECOND-FLOOR PLAN.

SERVANT'S ROOM
12 x 14

CLOS

HALL

CLOSET

DOWN

CHAMBER
14 x 16

CLOS

GRATE

HALL

GRATE

CHAMBER
15 x 16

HALL

LANDING

BAY

DOWN

GRATE

CLOSET

BATH ROOM
4 x 10

TUB

CHAMBER
15 x 18

FIRST-FLOOR PLAN.   SECOND-FLOOR PLAN.
PLAN No. 2—For Southern Requirements.

SIZE.

Plan No. 1, 27x48 feet, exclusive of steps.

Height of first story, 10 feet; second story, 9 feet, and is one and a half stories high.

Plan No. 2, 41 feet 6 inches x 66 feet, exclusive of steps.

Height of first and second stories, 10 feet each, full two stories.

Thickness of walls, 13 inches. Depth of cellar, 7 feet, under all up to hall.

OUTSIDE MATERIALS.

Foundation of stone. First and second stories brick. Roof slated. Outside blinds throughout. All wood work painted three coats.

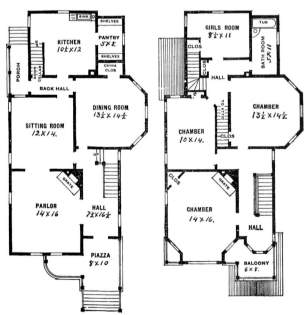

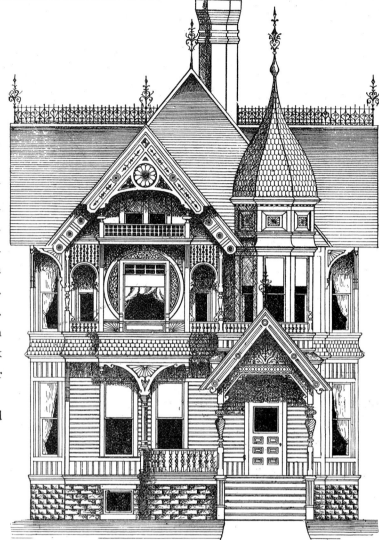

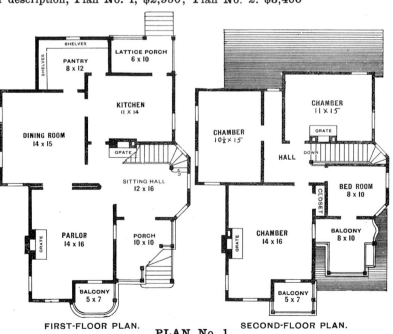

FRONT VIEW.

INTERIOR.

The vestibule, parlor, dining room and bed room are finished in hardwoods. Balance of house is painted work. Plastering, three-coat work, hard finish. Plumbing consists of sink and pump in kitchen, bath tub and bowls, with connections.

DESIGN No. 40.

SIZE.

Over all, except steps, 33 feet 6 inches x 46 feet 6 inches. Height of first story, 10 feet; second story, 9 feet 4 inches. Depth of cellar, 7 feet under all.

OUTSIDE MATERIALS.

First and second stories clapboarded, belts wainscoted, roof slated. Foundation, stone. Painting, three-coat work. Outside blinds throughout.

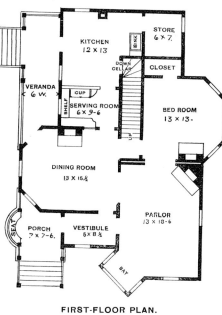

STORE
6 × 7.

KITCHEN
12 × 13

SINK

DOWN CELLAR

CLOSET

VERANDA
× 6 W. ×

CUP

SHELF

SERVING ROOM
6 × 9-6

BED ROOM
13 × 13.

DINING ROOM
13 × 15½

PORCH
7 × 7-6.

SEAT

VESTIBULE
5 × 8½

PARLOR
13 × 18-6

BAY

FIRST-FLOOR PLAN.

SERVANT'S ROOM
10 × 12

TRUNK ROOM
6 × 7.

CLOSET

CLOSET

TUB

BED

BATH ROOM
6 × 6.

CHAMBER
13 × 13½

HALL

CHAMBER
12 × 13.

BED

CLOSET

BED

CHAMBER
13 × 16½

BALCONY

SECOND-FLOOR PLAN.

PERSPECTIVE VIEW.

Residence of J. E. HATCH, Garrettsville, Ohio.

DESIGN No. 43.

NOTES.

In plan No. 2 we have the residence of Mr. J. E. Hatch, of Garrettsville, Ohio. It is a design that works up admirably in the building, presenting a much more tasty appearance than the illustration shows.

The rooms are of ample size and convenient. There are front and back stairs. The bath room is on the first floor and is reached from the bed room through a large closet.

The second story is convenient, each room being provided with ample closets. A hall extends through the house, connecting the front and back stairs and giving access to all the rooms. A narrow stairway leads to the attic. A tank is located in the rear of house, over the bath room.

(*See page 10.*)

SIZE.

Over all except steps—Plan No. 1, 41x66 feet; Plan No. 2, 34x46 feet. Height of first story—Plan No. 1, 10 feet 6 inches; second story, 9 feet 6 inches. Height of first story—Plan No. 2, 10 feet; second story, 9 feet 4 inches, Depth of cellar, 7 feet under all.

OUTSIDE MATE-RIALS.

First and second stories clapboarded, belts wainscoted, gables and roof shingled. Foundation of brick. Outside blinds. Painting, three-coat work.

SHELVES		SINK	TUB
PANTRY 5½ x 7			BATH ROOM 5½ x 7
SHELVES			

KITCHEN 11 x 18. CLOSET

PORCH 6 x 14 TO CELLAR BED ROOM 13 x 13

CHINA CLO.

DINING ROOM 12 x 16½

GRATE

HALL 6 x 13 PARLOR 13 x 15 BAY

PORCH 6 x 14

FIRST-FLOOR PLAN.

Tank

GIRLS ROOM 12 x 15 CLOSET

CLOSET HALL CHAMBER 13 x 13

CHAMBER 10 x 12 CLOSET

HALL CHAMBER 13 x 13 BALCONY

BALCONY 5 x 6

SECOND- FLOOR PLAN.

PLAN No. 2.

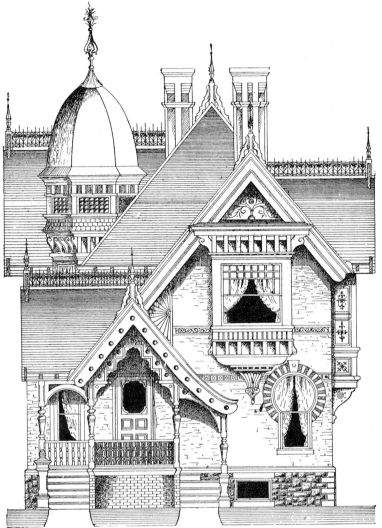

FRONT VIEW.

DESIGN No. 44.

Cost to build, as per description, Plan No. 1, $4,147; Plan No. 2, $5,350.

INTERIOR.

All of first story, except kitchen, is finished in hardwood; the rest in pine, for painting. Plastering, three-coat work, hard finish. Plumbing consists of sink and pump in kitchen, bath tub and bowl, with connections, gas throughout.

NOTES.

The price of this house can be varied by the quality of brick used. Those figured in the estimate are at $25 per thousand, but we would advise a better quality of pressed brick. The circular window in the hall bay is filled with plate glass. The bay could be partitioned off with glass and used as a conservatory with handsome effect. The Southern idea of arrangement is more plainly carried out in Plan No. 2, but either plan is well adapted to any climate.

These plans can be enlarged, reduced or changed to front in any desired direction.

(See page 10.)

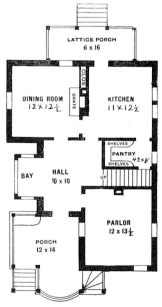

FIRST-FLOOR PLAN.

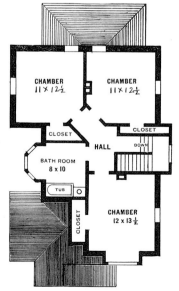

SECOND-FLOOR PLAN.

PLAN No. 1.

PERSPECTIVE VIEW.

DESIGN No. 45.

Cost to build, as per description, $3,550.

NOTES.

The exterior of this house is plainly finished, but its proportions and its broken-up appearance renders it a very attractive building. The veranda is commodious, the gable roof of which extends out over the steps, affording to them protection, as well as being a feature of considerable importance in the design. The roof balcony, entered through the dormer window from the attic, affords a splendid place for distant views.

The sitting hall is of ample size, has a neatly designed staircase with a large octagonal landing, which can be used for plants with handsome effect.

Every room in this house has been carefully studied and arranged with reference to convenience, any one of which can be entered from the hall in either story. The attic stairs go up over the back stairs and the cellar stairs under them.

Parlor and dining room can be connected by sliding doors, as the present arrangement is of Southern adaptation.

This plan can be enlarged, reduced or changed to front in any direction.

(*See page 10.*)

FRONT VIEW.

DESIGN No. 45.

INTERIOR.

Hall and parlor are finished in oak; balance of the rooms are to be painted three coats on pine or poplar finish. Plastering, three-coat work, hard finish. Plumbing consists of sink and pump in kitchen, bath tub and bowl, with connections, gas throughout.

SIZE.

Over all except steps, 41 feet x 60 feet 6 inches. Height of first story, 10 feet; second story, 9 feet 4 inches. Depth of cellar, 7 feet, under kitchen and back hall.

OUTSIDE MATERIALS.

First and second stories weatherboarded, belts wainscoted, gables shingled, roof shingled. Brick foundation. Outside blinds. Painting, three-coat work.

FIRST-FLOOR PLAN.   **SECOND-FLOOR PLAN.**

PERSPECTIVE VIEW.

DESIGN No. 46.

Cost to build, as per description, $3,480.

NOTES.

—

This is a modification of Plan No. 45. The rooms are somewhat smaller. The stair oriel is of different construction and has a much more elaborate exterior. It was designed for erection in the South, but can be modified to suit a colder climate by removing fireplaces (which are so largely used in a warm climate) and substituting sliding doors and using furnace or stove heat. The stair hall is a handsome feature, and should have the open fireplace, in any event. The bed-room grate is indispensable for ventilation and warmth in mild weather.

This plan can be enlarged, reduced or changed to front in any direction.

(*See page 10.*)

FRONT VIEW.

INTERIOR.

Parlor and hall are finished in oak or gum wood; dining room and bed room in bright pine; balance of house is finished for painting, three-coat work. Plastering, three-coat work, hard finish. Plumbing consists of sink and pump in kitchen and bath tub and bowl, with connections for all, gas throughout.

DESIGN No. 46.

SIZE.

Over all except steps, 39x50 feet. Height of first story, 10 feet; second story, 9 feet 4 inches. Depth of cellar, 7 feet, under all up to dining room.

OUTSIDE MATE-RIALS.

First and second stories clapboarded, belts wainscoted, gables and roof shingled Foundation of brick. Outside blinds. Painting, three-coat work.

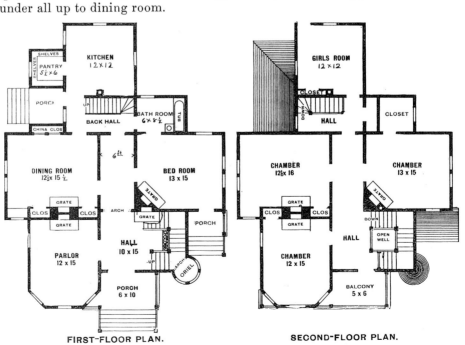

FIRST-FLOOR PLAN.   SECOND-FLOOR PLAN.

PERSPECTIVE VIEW.   *Residence of E. DEAN DOW, Knoxville, Tenn.*

DESIGN No. 47.

Cost to build, as per description, **Plan No. 1, $3,200; Plan No. 2, $4,000.**

SIZE.

Plan No. 1, 35x59 feet, exclusive of steps.

Plan No. 2, 39 feet 6 inches x 65 feet, exclusive of steps.

Height of first story, 10 feet 6 inches; second story, 10 feet.

Depth of cellar, 7 feet, under kitchen and back hall.

OUTSIDE MATERIALS.

First and second stories clapboarded, belts wainscoted, gables shingled and paneled, roof shingled. Foundation of brick. Outside blinds throughout. Painting, three-coat work.

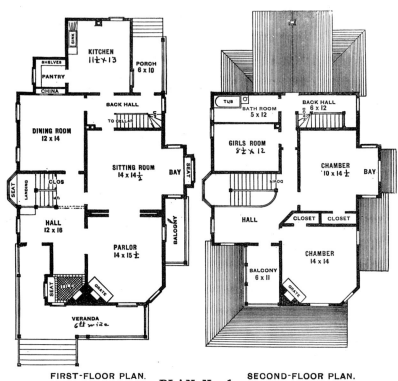

FIRST-FLOOR PLAN.   SECOND-FLOOR PLAN.

PLAN No 1.

NOTES.

This house has been recently erected upon Plan No. 2 at Knoxville, Tenn., by Mr. E. Dean Dow, and was arranged to suit the especial requirements of himself and wife in their declining years.

The rooms are ample, the ceilings of good height, stairs and all steps of easy ascent. If it is required to use family room for dining room the large closet can be made into a pantry and the present pantry into a bath room, and thus be reached from rear hall.

Our elevations were made from floor plans No. 1, which are considered quite a complete arrangement. A cozy reading nook is arranged in front end of hall, where the floor is laid in tile in front of fireplace. A neat arch cuts staircase off from main hall. The treatment of the rooms on both floors will be found to be both convenient and pleasant.

These plans can be enlarged, reduced or changed to front in any direction.

(*See page 10.*)

FRONT VIEW.

DESIGN No. 47.

INTERIOR.

Hall and parlor are finished in oak, dining room in cherry, family or sitting room in ash or gum wood. All the other rooms are to be treated to three coats of paint. Plastering, three-coat work, hard finish. Plumbing consists of sink and pump in kitchen, bath tub and bowl, with connections, and gas throughout.

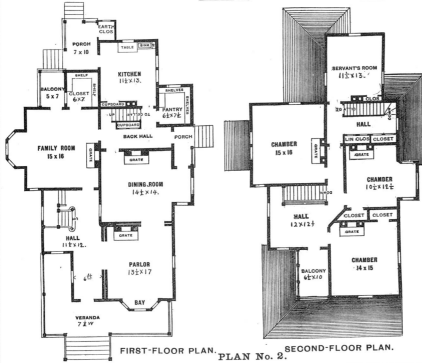

FIRST-FLOOR PLAN. PLAN No. 2. SECOND-FLOOR PLAN.

PERSPECTIVE VIEW.

DESIGN No. 48.

Cost to build, as per description, $5,400.

NOTES.

—

The ample veranda room in this design will be the delight of the owner. The hall is an attractive feature of this house. With the conservatory surrounding the circular landing its attractiveness can be imagined. The arrows indicate the course of the stairway to the second story, and seats are arranged on two landings in the flight. The entrance to the conservatory is from the landing on both front and back stairs. The passage around the conservatory between the shelves is 2 feet wide. The nook in dining room may be used for plants, if desired. The balcony over front veranda in front gable and in third story of tower adapts this design admirably to a river view, sea or lake-shore location. The attic, which is ample in size, may be finished off into rooms for any purpose. The more you study this plan the more you will get out of it.

This plan can be enlarged, reduced or changed to front in any desired direction.

(*See page 10.*)

FRONT VIEW.

DESIGN No. 48.

SIZE.

Over all except steps, 42x69 feet.

Height of first story, 10 feet 6 inches; second story, 10 feet.

Depth of cellar, 7 feet, under all.

OUTSIDE MATERIALS.

First story clapboarded, second story clapboarded and shingled above windows, gables shingled, belts wainscoted. Roof slated. Outside blinds throughout. Painting, three-coat work. Foundation walls of stone.

INTERIOR.

Parlor and reception room are finished in ash; hall and conservatory, antique oak; dining room in cherry; all natural finish. All other rooms to be finished in poplar, for painting or staining. Plastering, three-coat work, hard finish. Plumbing consists of sink and pump in kitchen, bath tub and bowl, with connections, and gas throughout.

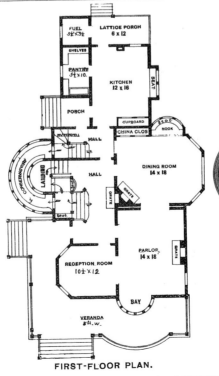

FIRST-FLOOR PLAN.

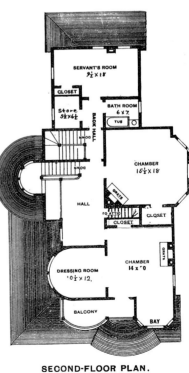

SECOND-FLOOR PLAN.

PERSPECTIVE VIEW.

DESIGN No. 49.

Cost to build, as per description, Plan No. 1, $3,450; Plan No. 2, $3,680.

NOTES.

In Plan No. 1 of this house (from which our perspective was made) we present a first-class residence of moderate size; the veranda being of especial importance, as it is large and occupies the entire front. That part in front of hall door is 12x13 feet. The hall is nice and contains a neat stairway, the landing of which is large and can be used as a receptacle for plants or other hall ornaments. A narrow hall leads through to the back porch and opens into all the rooms, which are well connected. The kitchen is cut off from main house and contains back and cellar stairs and opens into dining room through a serving room or pantry.

The second story has three good sleeping rooms, a bath and servant's room, with closets to all.

This plan can be enlarged, reduced or changed to front in any direction.

(See page 10.)

OUTSIDE MATERIALS.

First story weatherboarded, second story and gables shingled. Slate roof. Stone foundation. Cellar bottom cemented. Painting, three coats. Outside blinds. Galvanized iron gutters

INTERIOR.

Hall and parlor, oak finish; dining room, ash; balance of house paint work, three coats. Plastering, three-coat work, hard finish. Plumbing consists of sink and pump in kitchen, bath tub and bowl, with connections.

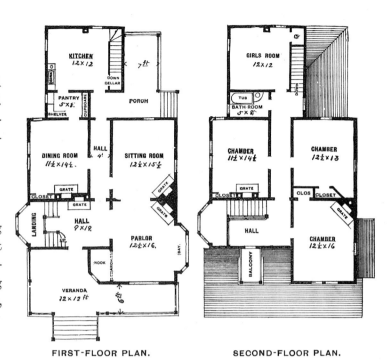

FIRST-FLOOR PLAN. **SECOND-FLOOR PLAN.**

PLAN No. 1.

SIZE.

Plan No. 1, 35x57 feet, exclusive of steps.   Plan No. 2, 38x50 feet, exclusive of steps.

Height of first story, 10 feet; second story, 9 feet 4 inches.   Depth of cellar, 7 feet, under all except hall and parlor.

FIRST-FLOOR PLAN. **SECOND-FLOOR PLAN.**

PLAN No. 2.

PERSPECTIVE VIEW.

DESIGN No. 50.

Cost to build, as per description, $4,287.

NOTES.

—

 We have in this house a rather imposing structure. The verandas and balconies are spacious and form a very important feature of the design. The hall is entered through a vestibule cut off from the main part by curtains. The vestibule extends back under the stairs to the landing, thus giving a good amount of cloak room. The dining room is 13x16 feet, has a large recessed fireplace, a spacious china closet and opens into both the back and front halls. The family room is large and has a deep bay window. A large closet or press is conveniently located near this room. The back hall contains a large dish cupboard and opens into the kitchen, dining and family rooms, pantry and side porch. A wide lattice porch is on the rear of kitchen. In the kitchen we have a large cupboard and access to the cellar, back stairs, pantry and side and rear entrances.

 The second story is well arranged, having large rooms, with closets, and all connecting with halls, which contain front, rear and attic stairs, and opening into bath room. Inside blinds throughout.

 This plan can be enlarged, reduced or changed to front in any direction.

(*See page 10.*)

FRONT VIEW.

DESIGN No. 50.

INTERIOR.

The hall, parlor, dining and family rooms on first floor, hall and front chamber on second floor are to be finished in hardwoods. All the rest paint work. Plastering, three-coat work, hard finish. Plumbing consists of sink and pump in kitchen, bath tub and bowl, with connections, gas throughout.

SIZE.

Over all except steps, 42x65 feet.

Height of stories, 10 feet 6 inches each.

Depth of cellar, 7 feet, under all.

OUTSIDE MATE-RIALS.

First and second stories clapboarded, belts wainscoted, gables shingled. Roof, slated. Foundation of stone. Painting, three-coat work.

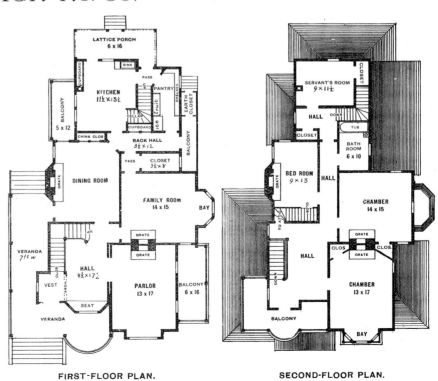

FIRST-FLOOR PLAN.

SECOND-FLOOR PLAN.

107

PERSPECTIVE VIEW.　　　　　　*DESIGN IN BRICK AND WOOD.*

DESIGN No. 51.

Cost to build, as per description, **Plan No. 1, $5,000; Plan No. 2, $6,500.**

SIZE.

Plan No. 1, 33x43 feet, exclusive of steps.　Plan No. 2, 35x56 feet, exclusive of steps.
Height of first story, 10 feet; second story, 9 feet 4 inches.　Depth of cellar, 7 feet, under all.

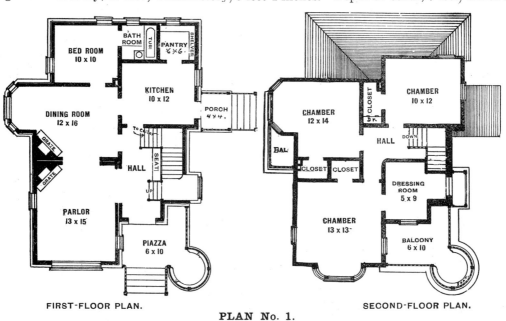

FIRST-FLOOR PLAN.　　　　　　　SECOND-FLOOR PLAN.

PLAN No. 1.

FRONT VIEW.

This house may have its first story solid wall or veneered with brick on a wood frame; the latter, in our estimation, being preferable. The large arched window is a very striking feature. Under the stone sill terra cotta blocks are used. The long side pieces are of polished marble, resting on carved stone bases supporting carved stone capitals, on which rests a beautiful arch of stone, alternated in colors. The spandrels or corners over the arch are filled with blue and pink glazed tile. With the bay window and gable balcony above, this treatment produces a very beautiful effect indeed. This residence was erected last season by Mr. J. H. Nelson, of Murfreesboro, Tenn., on a much larger scale, at a cost of $15,000, the first story being of stone, in two colors. The effect is very fine.

The floor plans are convenient and susceptible of many changes, and can be made to front in any direction.

(*See page 10.*)

DESIGN No. 51.

INTERIOR.

Hall, parlor and dining room finished in oak; balance of rooms to be of pine or poplar, painted. Plastering, three-coat work, hard finish. Plumbing consists of sink and pump in kitchen, bath tub and bowl, with connections, gas throughout.

OUTSIDE MATERIALS.

First story, brick; second story, shingled. Foundation, stone. Roof, slate. Painting, three-coat work. Outside blinds throughout.

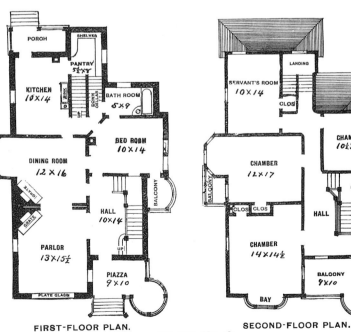

FIRST-FLOOR PLAN.   SECOND-FLOOR PLAN.

PLAN No. 2.

PERSPECTIVE VIEW.

STONE AND BRICK RESIDENCE.

DESIGN No. 52.

Cost to build, as per description, Plan No. 1, $5,100; Plan No. 2, $6,500.

SIZE.

Plan No. 1, 34x45 feet, over all.

Plan No. 2, 34x64 feet, over all.

Height of first story, 10 feet 6 inches; second story, 10 feet, in both plans.

Depth of cellar, 7 feet, under all.

OUTSIDE MATERIALS.

Foundation, brick, with stone facing above grade line. First story, stone facing, with brick backing; second story, brick, faced with pressed brick, at $25 per M. Belts and trimmings of stone, terra cotta and ornamental pressed brick. Gables of wood finish. Slate roof. Wood work painted three coats.

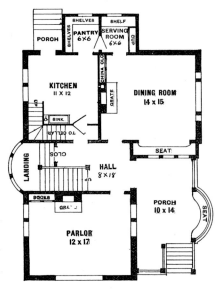

FIRST-FLOOR PLAN.

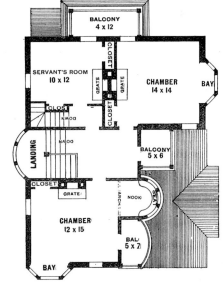

SECOND-FLOOR PLAN.

PLAN No. 1.

FRONT VIEW.

DESIGN No. 52.

INTERIOR.

Parlor and hall finished in cherry, dining and sitting rooms in ash; balance of house to be painted three coats, in desirable tints. Inside folding blinds throughout. Plastering, three-coat work, hard finish. Plumbing consists of sink and pump in kitchen, bath tub and bowl, with connections, gas throughout. Mantels, grates and hearths estimated at $310.

NOTES.

In this plan we present a stone and brick residence. The front veranda is broad and of artistic design. The parlor occupies the entire front and is large and well lighted with handsome plate and stained-glass windows. The hall contains a beautiful flight of stairs, and in Plan No. 1 the bath room is under the stair landing. The kitchen is separated from rest of house by a passage or hallway, and in each plan a pantry and serving room is provided. The chambers are all nice rooms, having good closets, and are provided with bays, nooks, balconies, &c., to render them cozy and comfortable, and at the same time assisting in the exterior effect.

These plans can be enlarged, reduced or changed to front in any direction.

(See page 10.)

FIRST-FLOOR PLAN. SECOND-FLOOR PLAN.

PLAN No. 2.

PERSPECTIVE VIEW.

DESIGN No. 53.

Cost to build, as per description, $5,250.

————

NOTES.

For a commodious house we invite close attention to the floor plans of this design. The front hall (with a handsome stairway) opens into the parlor, dining and family rooms and by a narrow passage into the back hall, which in turn opens out on to back porch, into kitchen, back stairs, family room, bath room and bed room.

The second story, besides having a beautiful hall, has three large chambers and a servant's. room, with ample closets to each, a large cedar closet and store room, also a convenient attic stairway.

In the family room bay window book cases, with glass doors, are built in either side. A pleasing change in this plan would be to omit the fireplaces and substitute sliding doors between parlor and dining room. The exterior is well proportioned and speaks for itself. The long veranda is richly finished and with its grand entrance way cannot fail to be admired by all. There is a plate-glass window in the hall, and the parlor bay has a horseshoe window, with plate and stained glass.

These plans can be enlarged, reduced or changed to front in any direction.

(*See page 10.*)

FRONT VIEW.

DESIGN No. 53.

INTERIOR.

Parlor and hall are finished in antique oak; sitting or family room, sycamore; dining room, ash or cherry; front chamber, chestnut. Balance of rooms are to be painted or stained as desired. Plastering, three-coat work, hard finish. Plumbing consists of sink and pump in kitchen, bath tub and bowl, with supply and waste pipe connections, gas throughout.

SIZE.

Over all except steps, 42 feet x 59 feet 6 inches.

Height of stories, 10 feet 6 inches each.

Depth of cellar, 7 feet, under all up to family and dining rooms.

OUTSIDE MATE-RIALS.

First and second stories clapboarded, belts shingled and wainscoted, gables shingled, roof slated. Iron cresting, galvanized iron gutters, &c. Outside blinds. Painting, three coats. Foundation walls stone, raised pointing.

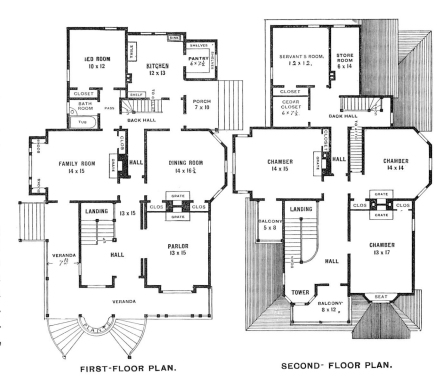

FIRST-FLOOR PLAN.

SECOND-FLOOR PLAN.

RIGHT PERSPECTIVE VIEW.

Residence of J. C. WHITE, Knoxville, Tenn.

DESIGN No. 54.

Cost to build, as per description, $3,500 to $3,800.

SIZE.

Over all except steps, 36x54 feet. Height of first story, 10 feet; second story, 9 feet 4 inches. Depth of cellar, 7 feet, under kitchen only.

OUTSIDE MATERIALS.

First and second stories weatherboarded, belt and gables shingled, roof slated. Foundation of brick. Painting, three-coat work. Outside blinds throughout.

LEFT PERSPECTIVE VIEW.

DESIGN No. 54.

Floor Plans shown on page 116.

INTERIOR.

The entire house is finished in what is known in the South as bright pine and in the North as hard or Georgia pine. It is treated to a coat of orange shellac, over which three coats of elastic varnish is applied, sandpapering each coat except the last. Plastering, three-coat work, hard finish. Plumbing consists of sink and pump in kitchen, bath tub and bowl, with waste and supply pipes, gas throughout.

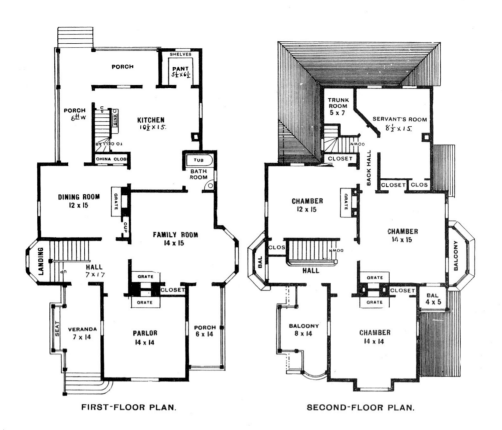

FIRST-FLOOR PLAN. SECOND-FLOOR PLAN.

FLOOR PLANS TO DESIGN NO. 54.

NOTES.

It will be noticed that the exterior of this design, for a moderate-sized house, is very striking and handsome. The porch and balcony treatment in the left perspective is richly constructed and of good proportions, the object being to get a handsome building at a moderate cost. The hall is neat and large enough for ordinary purposes, giving access to the parlor, family or sitting room and dining room. In the dining room there is a convenient closet, fitted with drawers and shelves, near the mantel, and a nice large china cupboard under back stairs, near kitchen door. The family room opens on to front porch and into kitchen, through a small bath room. There is also a nice closet and a large bay window, 9 feet wide. The kitchen contains back stairs, cellar way, a pantry and opens out on to a long porch. The second story is very convenient, giving fine rooms, with ample closets to all The front balcony is especially roomy.

This plan can be enlarged, reduced or changed to front in any direction.

(*See page 10.*)

PERSPECTIVE VIEW.

Residence of J. H. SETCHEL, Cuba, N. Y.

NOTES.

In this design we have a rather pleasant treatment of the veranda and balcony. The veranda ceiling, directly under the balcony floor, is recessed up 8 inches and beautifully paneled. The hall has an octagon end and forms a beautiful bay window in both stories. The three principal rooms open from the hall, and the bed room has a nice bath room and closet attached. The second story is provided with large closets and the front chamber is made very pleasant by the oriel window on the corner and the balcony opening from the side.

This plan can be enlarged, reduced or changed to front in any direction.

(See page 10.)

DESIGN No. 55.

Cost to build, as per description, **$4,000 to $4,500.**

SIZE.

Over all except steps, 39x47 feet. Height of first and second stories, 10 feet each. Depth of cellar, 7 feet under all.

OUTSIDE MATERIALS.

First and second stories weatherboarded, belts wainscoted, roof shingled. Foundation, stone. Painting, three-coat work. Outside blinds throughout.

INTERIOR.

Hall, parlor and sitting room finished in oak, all the rest painted three coats. Plastering, three-coat work, hard finish. Plumbing consists of sink and pump in kitchen, bath tub and bowl, with connections, gas throughout.

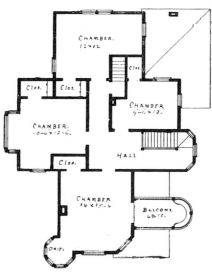

FIRST-FLOOR PLAN.

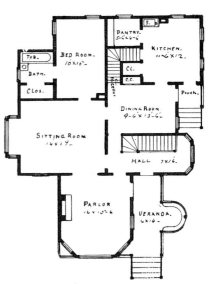

SECOND-FLOOR PLAN.

INTERIOR.

Parlor and hall finished in quartered oak; dining room, cherry or butternut; bed room, ash; balance pine, painted three coats. All painted work to be sandpapered after each coat except the last. Plastering, three-coat work, hard finish. Plumbing consists of sink and pump in kitchen, bath tub and bowl, with connections, and gas throughout.

SIZE.

Over all except steps, Plan No. 1, 38 feet 6 inches x 59 feet.

Height of first story, 10 feet 6 inches; height of second story, 9 feet.

Depth of cellar, 7 feet, under all.

LEFT PERSPECTIVE VIEW.   *Residence of D. J. EGLESTON, Knoxville, Tenn.*

DESIGN No. 56.

Cost to build, as per description, Plan No. 1, $3,900; Plan No. 2, $2,900.

OUTSIDE MATERIALS.

Entire body is clapboarded and painted in tints to bring out belts and other finishes. Roof slated. Foundation walls of brick, but stone would be much more suitable for a house of this kind. Painting, three-coat work, Outside blinds through out.

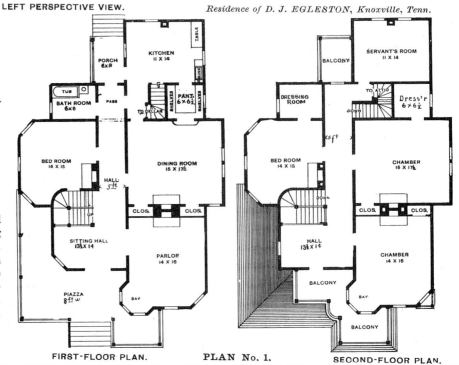

FIRST-FLOOR PLAN.   PLAN No. 1.   SECOND-FLOOR PLAN.

RIGHT PERSPECTIVE VIEW.

NOTES.

I cannot speak too strongly in regard to the attractiveness of this design.

The building itself looks fully 50 per cent. better than is shown in the engravings.

The veranda, balconies and open tower top present a magnificent appearance and affords such an opportunity for extensive views that the house is admirably adapted for a sea-side, lake-shore or river-view location.

Owing to a poor location for exposing the negative, the photograph does not show as good proportions in the building as it should.

The staircase in front hall is shown on page 120, engraved direct from photograph.

This plan can be enlarged, reduced or changed to front any desired direction.

(*See page 10.*)

DESIGN No. 56.

SIZE.

Over all except steps, Plan No. 2, 36 feet x 49 feet 6 inches.

Height of stories and outside materials same as in plan No. 1.

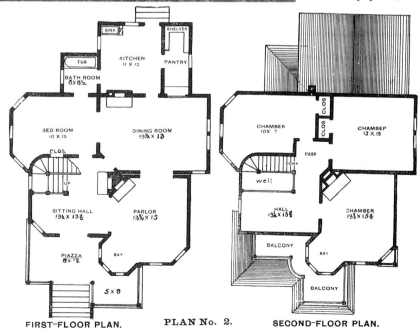

FIRST-FLOOR PLAN.   PLAN No. 2.   SECOND-FLOOR PLAN.

DESIGN No. 57.

The above engraving is a view of hall staircase in the residence of D. J. Egleston, views of which are shown on pages 118 and 119. The above case is constructed in oak, finished antique. The small rosettes shown throughout the work are of tinted embossed tile of handsome pattern, and a very beautiful effect is obtained by their use.

DESIGN No. 58.

NOTE.

On this page we present a view of staircase and hall in the residence of Mr. Wm. Weiss, at Beaumont, Texas, elevation of which is shown on page 88, and was erected from my plans by the Reliance Lumber Company, of which Mr. Weiss is President. The climate of this section of the country requires peculiar arrangement and construction in residence work for healthfulness and durability, points which we observe in all our working plans.

PERSPECTIVE VIEW.

DESIGN No. 59.

Cost to build, as per description, $4,800.

NOTES.

We have in this design what is considered a handsome and well-proportioned house—one suited to a location having extensive views. The veranda is commodious and opens into hall and sitting room. The back or side hall contains back stairs and cellar way, opens into kitchen, dining room and out on to side porch. There is another back hall or passage leading from sitting room to rear porch and opens into bed and bath rooms. The arrangement of front part is convenient, rooms large and well lighted. The second story is convenient, rooms all having good closets and are entered from hall. The tower is square at first story, octagonal at second and round at the third and roof. The oriel on right side adds to the effect of the exterior.

This house is susceptible of many changes.

(*See page 10.*)

FRONT VIEW.

OUTSIDE MATERIALS.

First and second stories weather-boarded, belt shingled, gable shingled, roof slated. Foundation, brick. Painting, three coats. Outside blinds.

INTERIOR.

Hall, parlor, dining and sitting rooms are to be finished in oak or other hardwoods. Balance of rooms to be of pine or poplar finish and painted three coats. Plastering, three-coat work, hard finish. Plumbing consists of sink and pump in kitchen, bath tub and bowl, with connections, gas throughout.

DESIGN No. 59.

SIZE.

Over all except steps, 44 feet 6 inches x 66 feet.

Height of first story, 11 feet; second story, 10 feet.

Depth of cellar, 7 feet, under all except parlor and hall.

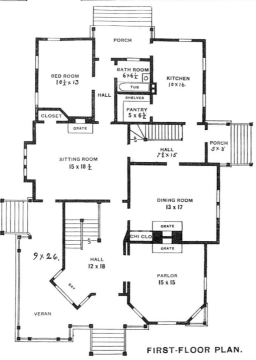

FIRST-FLOOR PLAN.

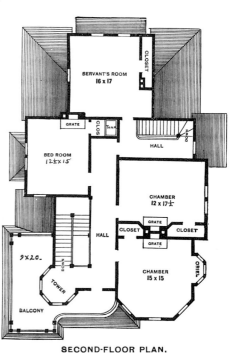

SECOND-FLOOR PLAN.

INTERIOR.

Dining room, hall, library and parlor in hardwood, natural finish. All other rooms painted three-coat work. Plastering, three-coat work, hard finish. Plumbing consists of sink and pump in kitchen, bath tub and bowl, with connections, gas throughout.

SIZE.

Plan No. 1, 36x48 feet 6 inches.

Height of first story, 10 feet 6 inches; second story, 9 feet 4 inches.

Depth of cellar, 7 feet, under all except library and parlor.

PERSPECTIVE VIEW.   *Residence of GEO. F. BARBER, Knoxville, Tenn.*

DESIGN No. 60.

Cost to build, as per description, **Plan No. 1**, $3,300; **Plan No. 2**, $3,850.

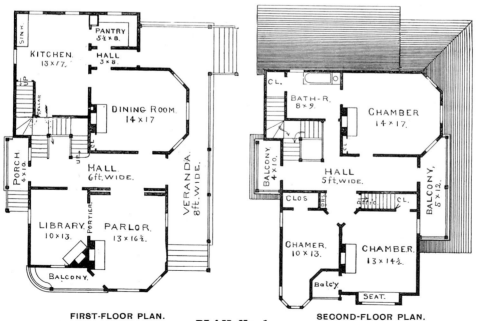

FIRST-FLOOR PLAN.   **PLAN No. 1.**   SECOND-FLOOR PLAN.

OUTSIDE MATE-RIALS.

First and second stories clapboarded, belts shingled and wainscoted, gables shingled, roof slated. Outside blinds throughout. Painting, three-coat work. Foundation walls of brick.

FRONT VIEW.

DESIGN No. 60.

NOTES.

The design is novel yet very attractive, and has become a general favorite among all lovers of true art in architecture. The stairway is of neat design, and is an attractive feature of front hall. Door under stairs leads from the hall into kitchen.

This building itself looks much better than is shown in the engravings.

This plan can be enlarged, reduced or changed to front in any desired direction.

(*See page 10.*)

SIZE.

Plan No. 2, 44x55½ feet, over all except steps.

Height of stories and cellar, same as Plan No. 1.

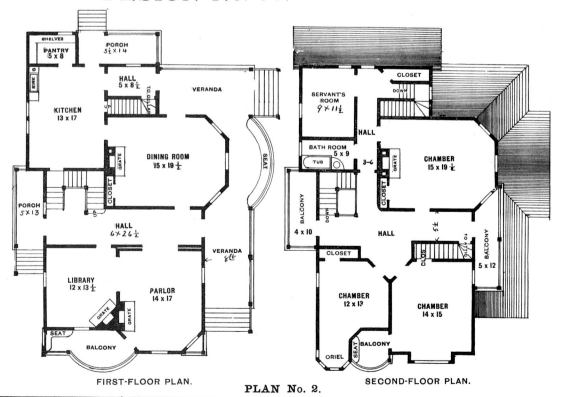

FIRST-FLOOR PLAN.

PLAN No. 2.

SECOND-FLOOR PLAN.

FRONT VIEW.

DOUBLE TENEMENT HOUSE.

NOTES.

In this design we present a two-story double tenement house. There is a slight difference in the plan arrangement of the two sides, but they are essentially the same. Each side has a vestibule, separated from the main hall by an arch and curtains. The hall contains the stairs and opens into parlor and dining room. Each dining room is provided with a bay window, a large closet and a china cupboard. The pantry is convenient, separates the dining room from the kitchen and is to be used as a serving room. The back stairs and cellar way are conveniently arranged in the kitchen and a fuel room opens off from back porch. A double partition wall extends up through the building and serves as a deadener of sound. The second story is convenient, all the rooms having good closets. The hall admits to all chambers and contains front, back and attic stairs.

The exterior is plain yet pleasing in design.

Any other styles made to order. This plan can be enlarged, reduced or changed to suit.

(*See page 10.*)

DESIGN No. 61.

Cost to build, as per description, $4,500.

SIZE.

Over all except steps, 47 x 65 feet. Height of first and second stories, 10 feet each. Depth of cellar, 7 feet, under kitchens.

OUTSIDE MATERIALS.

First and second stories weatherboarded, belts wainscoted, roof shingled. Foundation, brick. Painting, three coats. Outside blinds.

INTERIOR.

The entire interior finish is to be painted three coats, smooth work. The halls, parlors and dining rooms could be finished in hardwoods with good effect. Plastering, three coats, hard finish. Plumbing consists of sink and pump in kitchens, bath tubs and bowls, with connections, gas throughout.

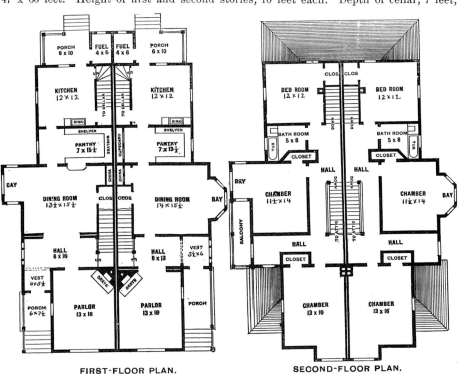

FIRST-FLOOR PLAN.

SECOND-FLOOR PLAN.

PERSPECTIVE VIEW.

VILLAGE BARN.

SIZE.

Over all, 22x32 feet 6 inches.

Carriage room, 12x 21 feet.

Height of first story, 9 feet, second story, 8 feet.

OUTSIDE MATE-RIALS.

Body of building weatherboarded, gables and roof shingled. Foundation of brick. Painting, three-coat work.

DESIGN No. 62.

Cost to build, as per description, $650.

NOTES.

In this plan we present a design for a convenient and tasty barn. Proportion, more than ornamentation, has been the aim in the exterior appearance. The interior has four good stalls, to be used as desired, on first floor, and the second story can be used for hay and grain and a man's room can be partitioned off if wanted, and have plenty of room left. Chutes are arranged to carry hay and grain from above.

Any desired changes can be made in this plan.

(*See page 10.*)

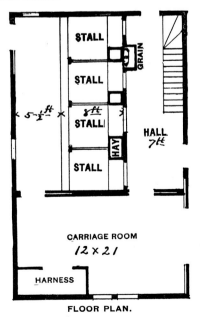

FLOOR PLAN.

PERSPECTIVE VIEW.

CITY BARN.

DESIGN No. 63.

SIZE.

Over all, 32 feet 6 inches x 39 feet.

Height of first story, 8 feet; second story, up to rafters.

OUTSIDE MATERIALS.

The entire structure is weatherboarded up to eaves. Gables and roof shingled. Foundation, stone. Painting, three-coat work.

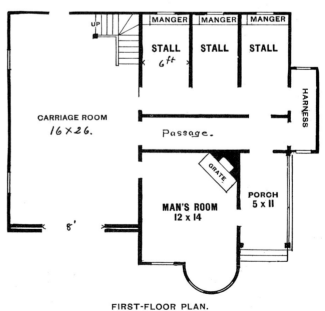

FIRST-FLOOR PLAN.

FRONT VIEW.

DESIGN No. 63.

Cost to build, as per description, $1,000 to $1,200.

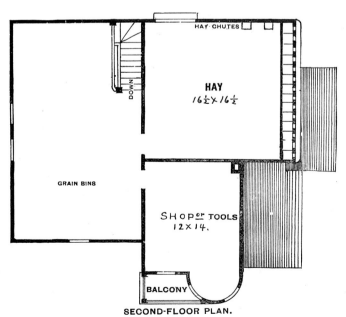

SECOND-FLOOR PLAN.

NOTES.

This was designed for a city or village barn; to have ample and convenient floor space, to be neat and artistic in appearance and at as small an outlay as possible.

The man's room is in front and has good outlooks. It can be entered from porch or carriage room. A grate in the corner will afford heat in cold weather, and a couch can be placed in the opposite corner for sleeping purposes. The passage cuts the stalls off from main part of barn, and the harness room is conveniently located. A nice shop is over the man's room, for boys to work in. Other parts of the second story can be arranged for hay or grain, as required.

This plan can be enlarged, reduced or changed to front in any direction.

(*See page 10.*)

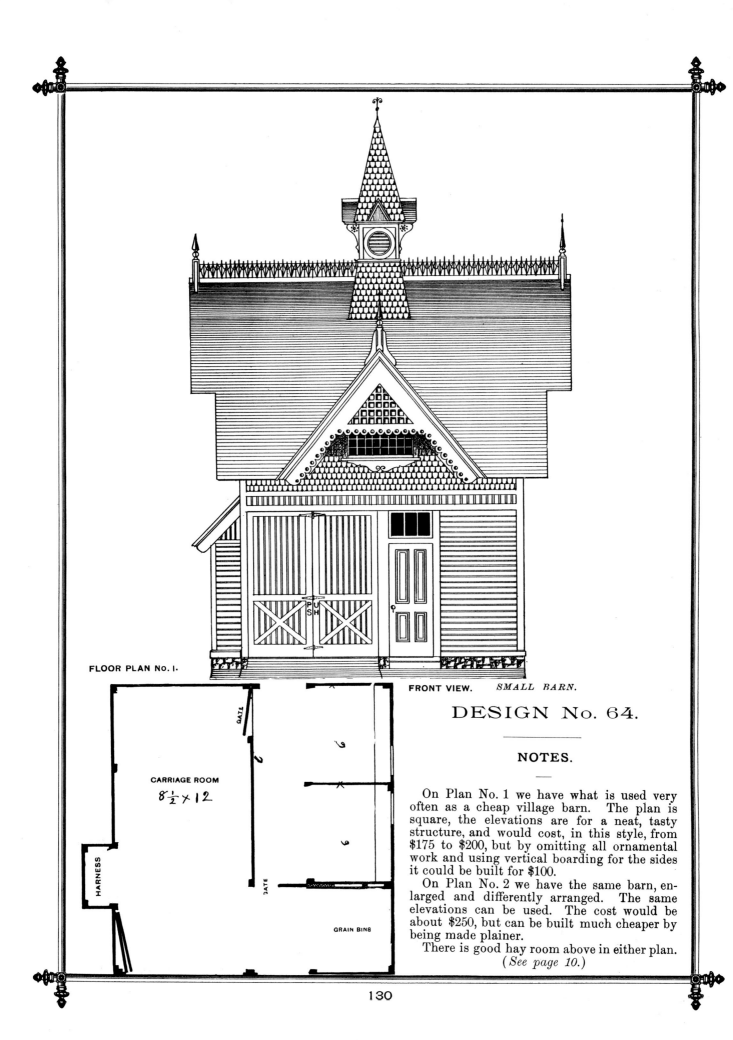

FLOOR PLAN No. 1.

FRONT VIEW.   SMALL BARN.

CARRIAGE ROOM
$8\frac{1}{2} \times 12$

HARNESS

GATE

GRAIN BINS

DESIGN No. 64.

NOTES.

On Plan No. 1 we have what is used very often as a cheap village barn. The plan is square, the elevations are for a neat, tasty structure, and would cost, in this style, from $175 to $200, but by omitting all ornamental work and using vertical boarding for the sides it could be built for $100.

On Plan No. 2 we have the same barn, enlarged and differently arranged. The same elevations can be used. The cost would be about $250, but can be built much cheaper by being made plainer.

There is good hay room above in either plan.

(*See page 10.*)

END VIEW. *SMALL BARN.*

DESIGN No. 64.

SIZE.

Plan No. 1, 18x18 feet. Plan No. 2, 18x30 feet. Height of story, 8 feet studding, 12 feet.

OUTSIDE MATERIALS.

The body, up to roof, is weatherboarded, gables and roof shingled. Painting, three coats.

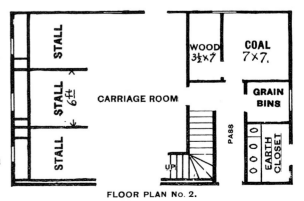

FLOOR PLAN No. 2.

PERSPECTIVE VIEW.   *FRAME CHAPEL.*

DESIGN No. 65.

Cost to build, as per description, Plan No. 1, $2,150; Plan No. 2, $4,700.

NOTES.

The price given is for the building alone, and does not include furniture, seating or heating apparatus.

In Plan No. 1 the seats and furniture can be made to cost from $150 to $300, and in Plan No. 2 from $350 to $600. A furnace for heating would cost from $175 to $250. The walls and ceiling are to be plastered two coats, brown mortar, and left under the float when perfectly dry to be painted three coats in tints. Inexpensive open timber work shows below the ceiling.

The ceiling is provided with ornamental registers or openings in apex for ventilation. The registers are kept closed during services and opened as soon as audience is dismissed, when the vitiated air immediately and effectually escapes, as the registers are in the highest point of the room. All the interior wood work is to be of pine, grained to imitate oak and cherry trimmings. The glass in the windows is to be ordinary cathedral, in squares, but more handsome patterns would be desirable.

These plans can be enlarged, reduced or changed to front in any direction.

(*See page 10.*)

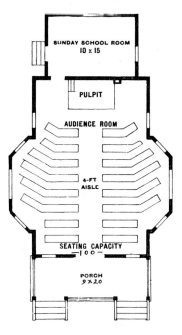

FLOOR PLAN No. I.

SUNDAY SCHOOL ROOM
10 x 15

PULPIT

AUDIENCE ROOM

4-FT
AISLE

SEATING CAPACITY
— 100 —

PORCH
9 x 20

SIZE.

Plan No. 1, 28x47 feet 6 inches.
Studding, 15 feet long. Height
to top of belfry, 47 feet.

Plan No. 2, 42x68 feet. Other
dimensions in proportion. Basement for furnace only.

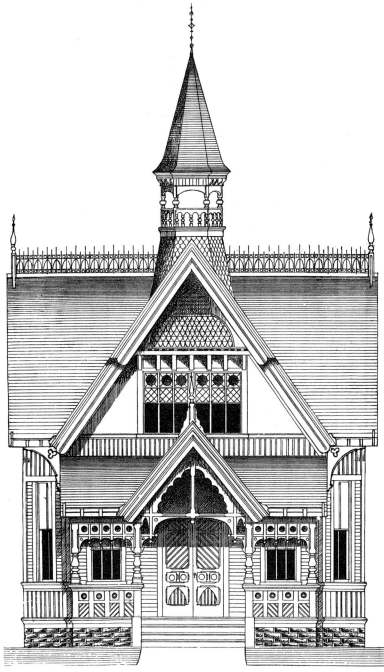

FRONT VIEW.

DESIGN No. 65.

OUTSIDE MATERIALS.

The front view exterior is shown to be of weatherboarding, but
in the perspective view it is of vertical boarding, in gothic panels,
and a very appropriate and artistic treatment. Gables, timbered
and shingled. Roof, shingled. Foundation, stone.

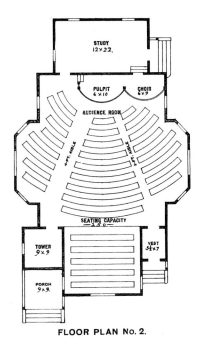

STUDY
12 x 22

PULPIT
6 x 10

CHOIR
6 x 9

AUDIENCE ROOM

4-FT. AISLE

SEATING CAPACITY
— 250 —

TOWER
9 x 9

VEST
5½ x 7

PORCH
9 x 9

FLOOR PLAN No. 2.

PERSPECTIVE VIEW.   *FRAME CHURCH.*

DESIGN No. 66.

Cost to build, as per description, **Plan No. 1, $4,000; Plan No. 2, $6,500.**

NOTES.

    This is a more pretentious and elaborate building than the one shown on page 132, but the same general description will answer for both. There is a neat corner tower, serving in its first story as a vestibule and in its second story as a belfry. (Bell not included in estimate.) The walls and ceiling are plastered and are to be painted in tints. Open timber work hangs below the ceiling, to be grained in imitation of oak, as is all the wood work of this design. Two hundred and fifty dollars is allowed for glass in the large front window, and all other windows to have neatly-designed art glass.

    We invite correspondence concerning these or any other class of church buildings.

(See page 10.)

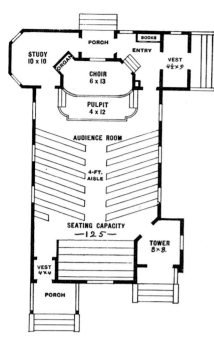

FLOOR PLAN No. 1.

SIZE.

Over all except steps, 32 feet 6 inches x 45 feet.

Side walls are 15 feet high. Spire, 61 feet.

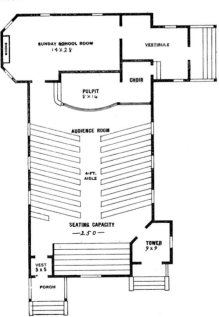

FLOOR PLAN No. 2.

SIZE.

Over all except steps, 45 feet 6 inches x 61 feet.

The height is in proportion to its other dimensions.

FRONT VIEW.

DESIGN No. 66.

OUTSIDE MATERIALS.

Clapboarding is used to the top of the windows. Above this it is shingled. Roof, shingled. Foundation of stone. No basement is included in the estimate.

FRONT VIEW.
THREE-STORY STORE FRONT.

DESIGN No. 67.

NOTES.

The width of this building is 30 feet. Height of stories 12 feet, 11 feet and 11 feet. There are no plans given, owing to the fact that each individual's requirements are so different, length of lot, use to which each story is to be put and amount of money to be involved. The second and third stories may be used for offices or fitted up in tasty living apartments.

Parties who would like to build from these designs can correspond with us, giving size of lot and use the several floors are to be put to, and we will send sketches of floor plans to suit individual wants.

Materials used are iron, brick, stone and terra cotta.

(See page 10.)

FRONT VIEW. *TWO-STORY STORE FRONT.*

DESIGN No. 68.

NOTES.

The same description answers for this design as for No. 67 except that this is for a 25-foot lot. Two stories, each 12 feet high. The building may be made three or more stories high, as required.

We can furnish artistic designs for store buildings of any size. We only ask you to state your wants.

(See page 10.)

PERSPECTIVE VIEW.　　　　　SUMMER HOUSE.

DESIGN No. 69.

The illustrations on this page are for an artistic pavilion or summer house. It can be used with good effect in a park or on private grounds. The size and shape of the plan renders it an excellent building for a band stand for summer concerts.

There are many uses to which this building can be put with good effect.

Size of plan is 12 feet wide and 18 feet long. Price, from $250 to $350.

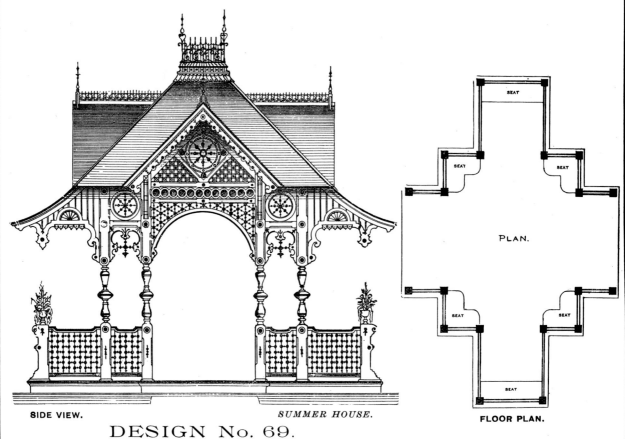

SIDE VIEW.　　　　　SUMMER HOUSE.

DESIGN No. 69.

FLOOR PLAN.

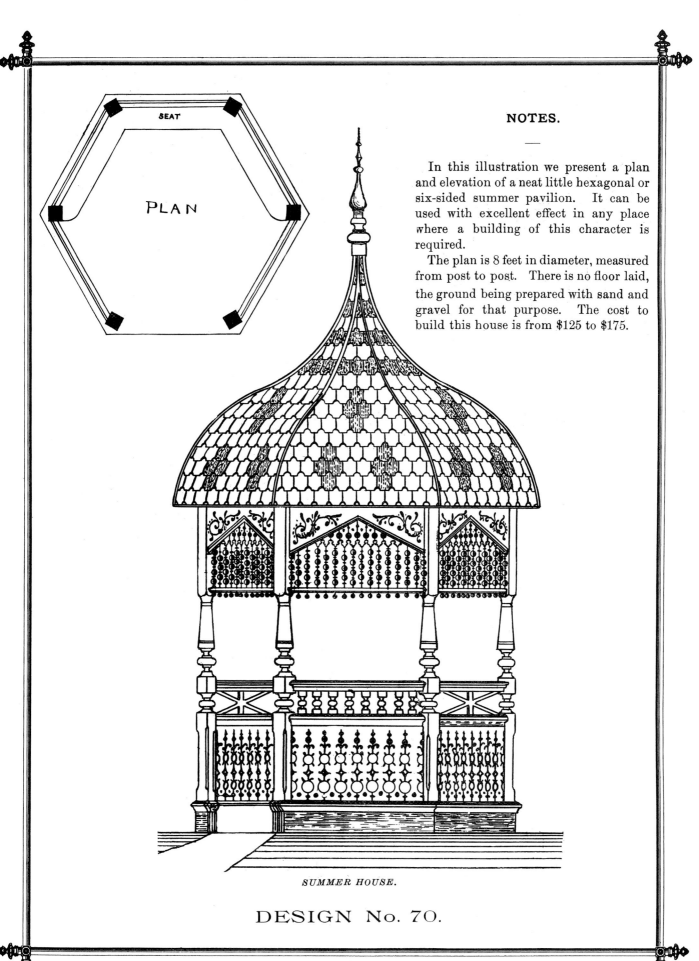

PLAN

SEAT

In this illustration we present a plan and elevation of a neat little hexagonal or six-sided summer pavilion. It can be used with excellent effect in any place where a building of this character is required.

The plan is 8 feet in diameter, measured from post to post. There is no floor laid, the ground being prepared with sand and gravel for that purpose. The cost to build this house is from $125 to $175.

SUMMER HOUSE.

DESIGN No. 70.

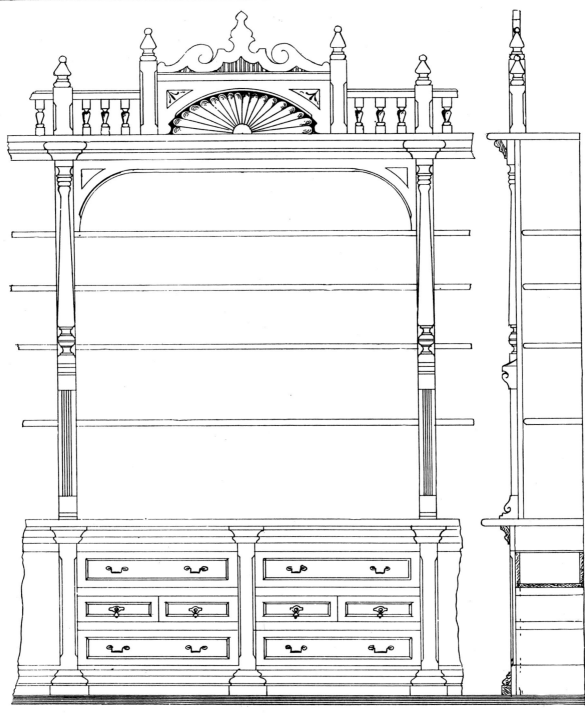

FRONT.   *STORE SHELVING.*   SECTION.

DESIGN No. 71.

NOTE.

This design is suitable for a drug, jewelry or confectionery store.   The drawers below can be cut up in sizes to suit.   Scale, $\frac{3}{4}$ inch = 1 foot.

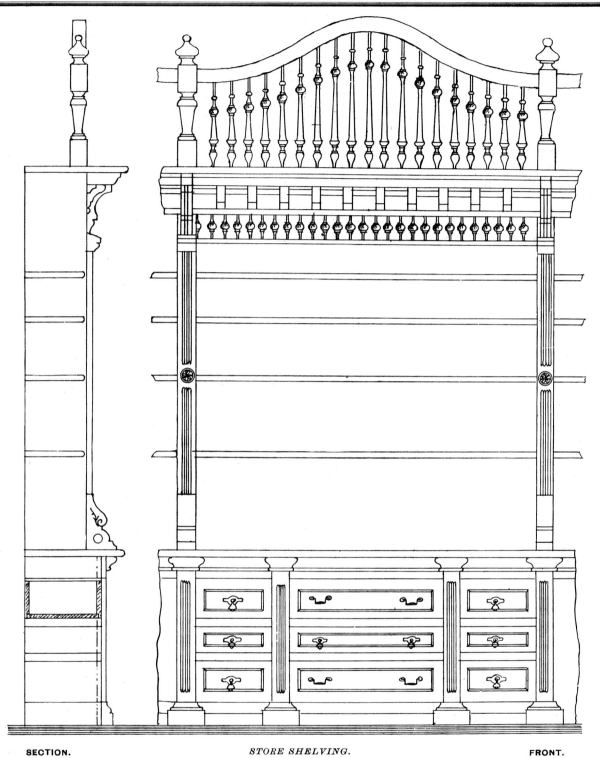

SECTION.   *STORE SHELVING.*   FRONT.

DESIGN No. 72.

NOTE.

This shows another design for store shelving, and can be used very appropriately in the same kind of stores as that shown in No. 71 and in a store used for almost any purpose. Scale, ¾ inch = 1 foot.

COUNTER.

DESIGN No. 73.

COUNTER.

DESIGN No. 74.

NOTE.

The two designs on this page are for inexpensive counters. They can be used in any kind of a store where very nice work is not required. The rosettes shown in No. 73 are pressed-wood ornaments, set in.

WALL CABINET.

DESIGN No. 75.

NOTE.

This very neat wall cabinet was recently built by a young man here at a cost of about $12. The wood work is poplar, stained oak. The shaded panels are beveled plate mirrors; the others are either carved or pressed-wood ornaments. The circle doors inclose a case with plain glass sides, so that the contents can be seen from sides or front. Scale, ¾ inch = 1 foot.

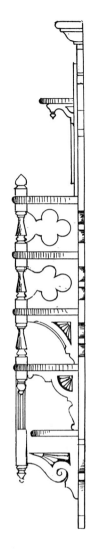

WALL CABINET.

DESIGN No. 76.

NOTE.

In this is given another design for a very tasty wall cabinet. The center panel is a beveled plate mirror. The two panels above are for photographs. The six panels at the side are for pressed-wood ornaments. All others are hand-carved. This could be made to stand on the floor or on a table by adding a base or legs to it. Scale, $\frac{3}{4}$ inch = 1 foot.

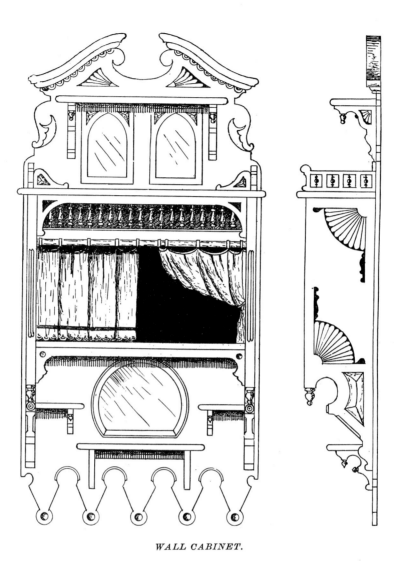

WALL CABINET.

DESIGN No. 77.

NOTE.

We give in this a third design for a wall cabinet and book case combined. That part shown with curtains is for books, the other shelves are for bric a brac. The two gothic panels above are for either photographs or mirrors. These three designs will be found to work up into very handsome pieces of furniture. Scale, $\frac{3}{4}$ inch = 1 foot.

BAY WINDOW (FRONT AND SIDE.)

DESIGN No. 78.

NOTE.

In this is given a design for an octagon bay window. The corners of the roof are carried out square and supported by brackets. A neat balustrade surmounts the roof, forming a small balcony. For scale, see No. 79.

BAY WINDOW (FRONT AND SIDE.)

DESIGN No. 79.

NOTE.

A design for a square bay window. Can be added to almost any cottage, and will be found to work up handsomely. See scale at top.

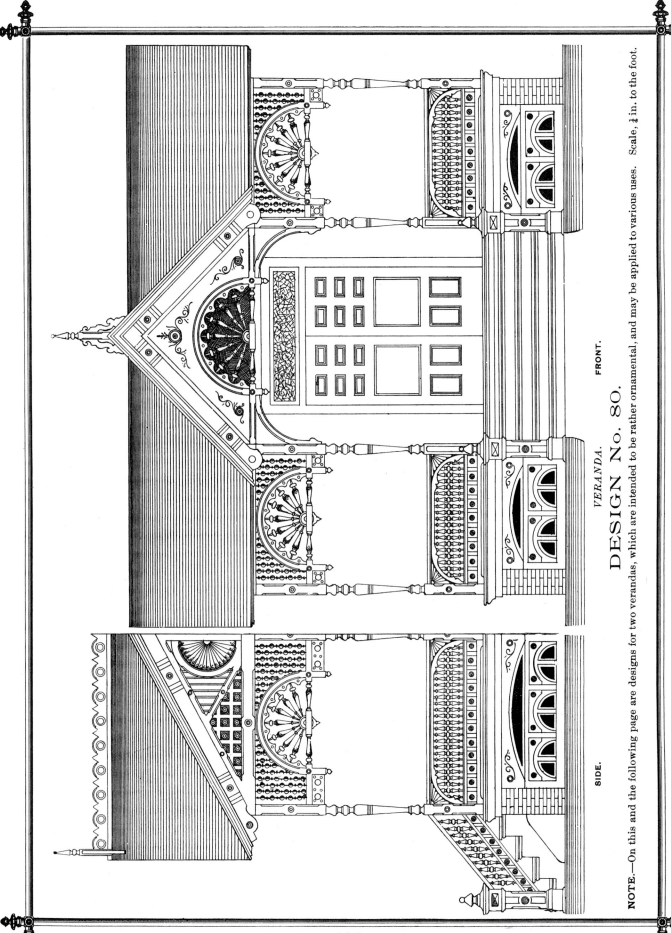

VERANDA. FRONT.

SIDE.

DESIGN No. 80.

NOTE.—On this and the following page are designs for two verandas, which are intended to be rather ornamental, and may be applied to various uses. Scale, ¼ in. to the foot.

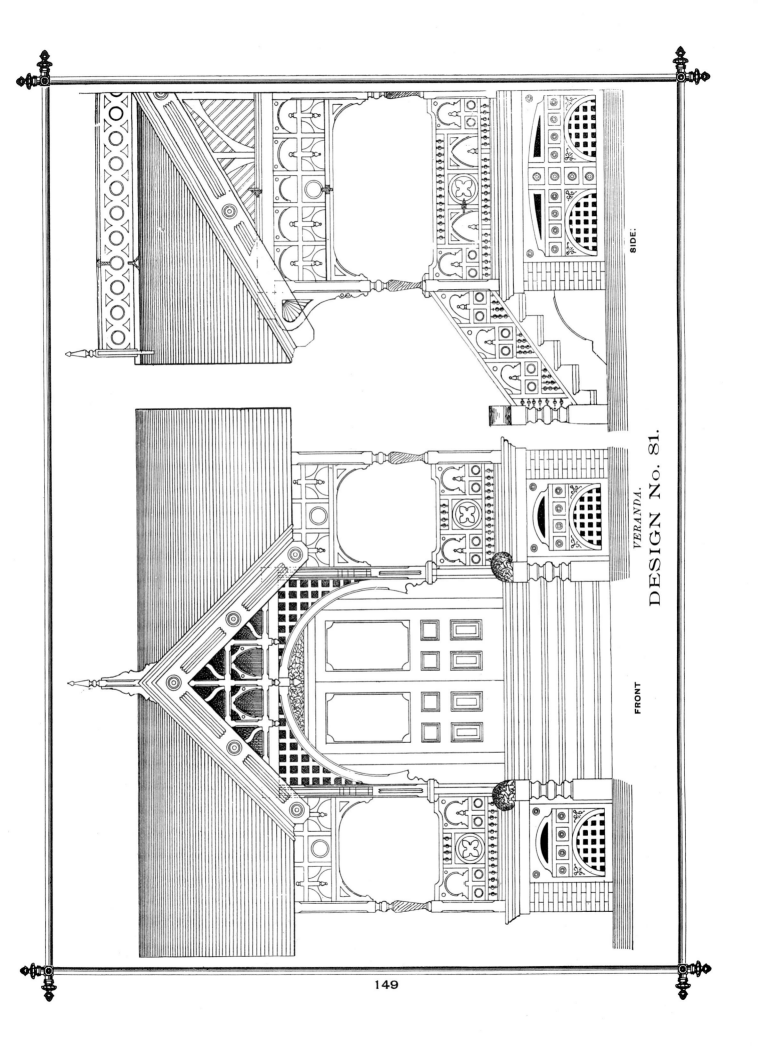

VERANDA.

DESIGN No. 81.

SIDE.

FRONT

VERANDA.   *VERANDA.*

DESIGN No. 82.   DESIGN No. 83.

NOTE.

    This page shows end view of two porticos, or which may be lengthened into verandas. These designs are given for the benefit of those who would like them separate from house designs.

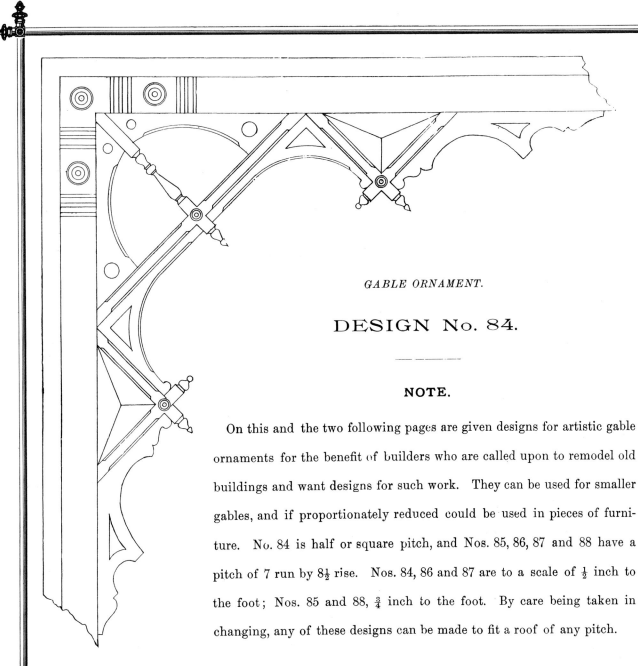

GABLE ORNAMENT.

DESIGN No. 84.

NOTE.

On this and the two following pages are given designs for artistic gable ornaments for the benefit of builders who are called upon to remodel old buildings and want designs for such work. They can be used for smaller gables, and if proportionately reduced could be used in pieces of furniture. No. 84 is half or square pitch, and Nos. 85, 86, 87 and 88 have a pitch of 7 run by 8½ rise. Nos. 84, 86 and 87 are to a scale of ½ inch to the foot; Nos. 85 and 88, ¾ inch to the foot. By care being taken in changing, any of these designs can be made to fit a roof of any pitch.

GABLE ORNAMENT.

DESIGN No. 85.

GABLE ORNAMENT.

DESIGN No. 86.

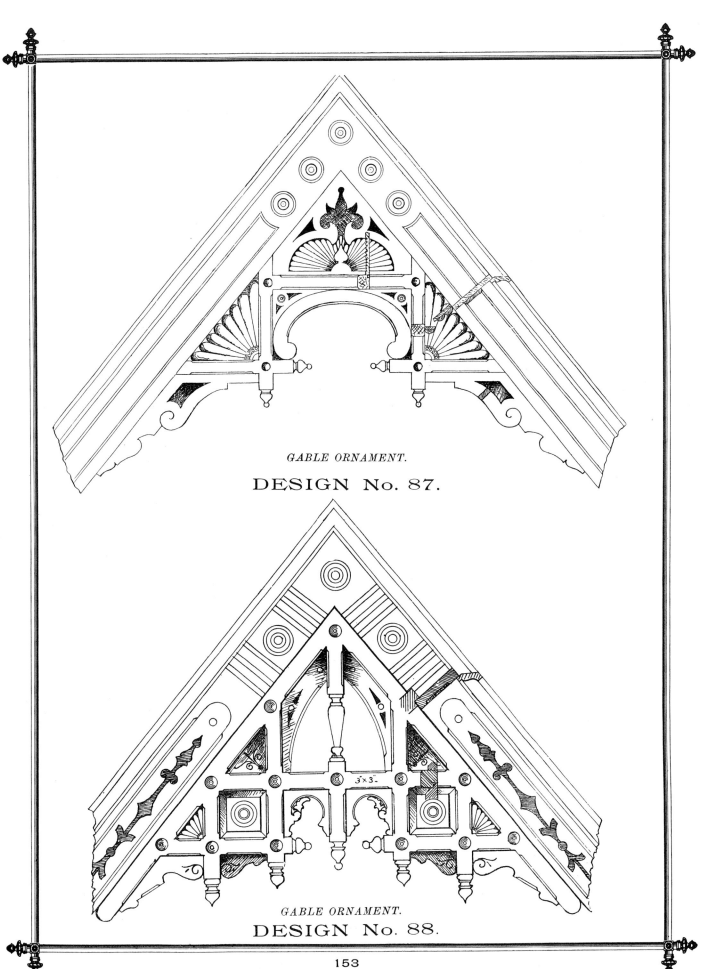

GABLE ORNAMENT.

DESIGN No. 87.

GABLE ORNAMENT.

DESIGN No. 88.

No. 90 is a staircase design, used in the residences shown on pages 14 and 121, and is considered a very neat thing for a residence of this price. It is applicable to any house having a 11-foot story. Scale, 1 inch to the foot.

SECTION OF STAIRCASE.

DESIGN No. 89.

—

NOTE.

—

No. 89 is a design for a staircase, which can be executed in any kind of wood. It is the one used in the residence shown on page 118 and the hall on page 120. Scale, 1 inch to the foot.

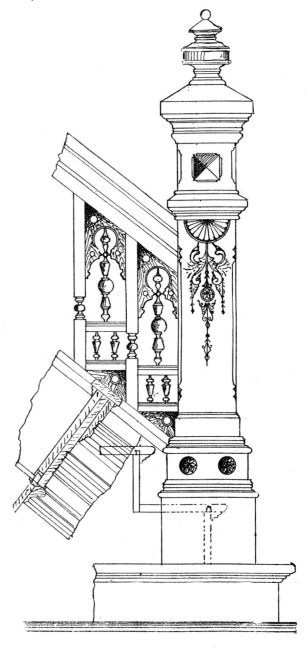

SECTION OF STAIRCASE.

DESIGN No. 90.

NOTE.

—

No. 91 was designed for house shown on page 122, and is a very neat case, costing from $150 to $225, according to plan and woods used.

Any of these cases can be changed to fit any house desired.

Scale, 1 inch to the foot.

SECTION OF STAIRCASE.

DESIGN No. 91.

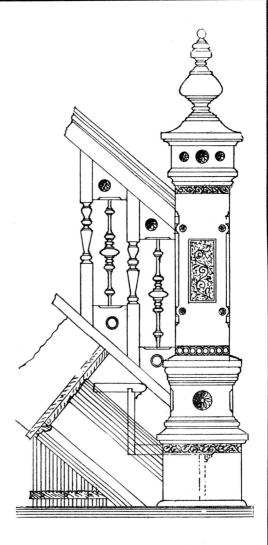

SECTION OF STAIRCASE.

DESIGN No. 92.

NOTE.

—

No. 92 shows the stair case used in the residence on page 124, and can be built in hard pine for $75 to $100. It works up very beautifully and attracts especial attention. The drawings are made for a 10 foot 6 inch story, but may be changed to a story of any height. Scale, 1 inch to the foot.

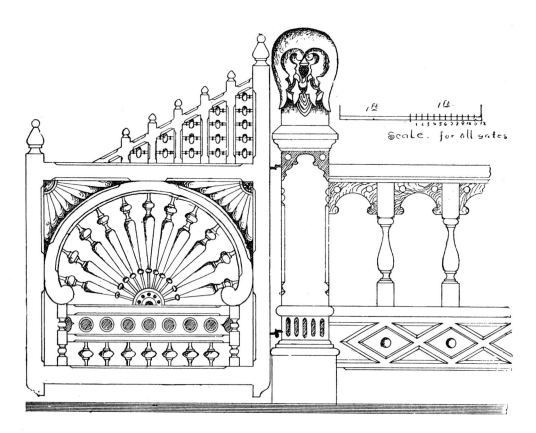

GATE.

DESIGN No. 93.

NOTE.

—

On pages 156, 157, 158 and 159 are given designs for gates, gate posts and fences, for the benefit of mechanics wanting such designs and for individuals, from which to select a design for a front gate or an ornamental fence for enclosing their premises.

Our aim has not been to give plain or ordinary designs, such as any mechanic can build, but new and somewhat artistic designs, such as are not to be seen elsewhere.

No attempt at price has been made, as any mechanic can give their local cost of such work, the details all being drawn to a scale of $\frac{3}{4}$ inch to the foot.

GATE.

DESIGN No. 94.

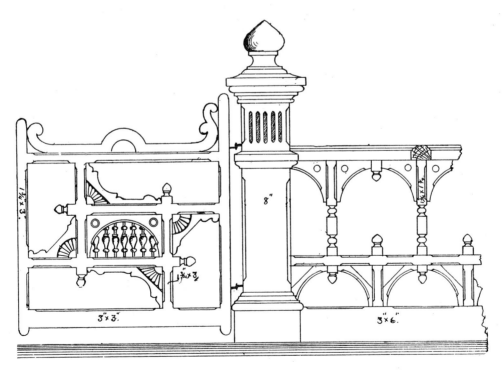

GATE.

DESIGN No. 95.

GATE.   *FENCE.*

DESIGN No. 96.

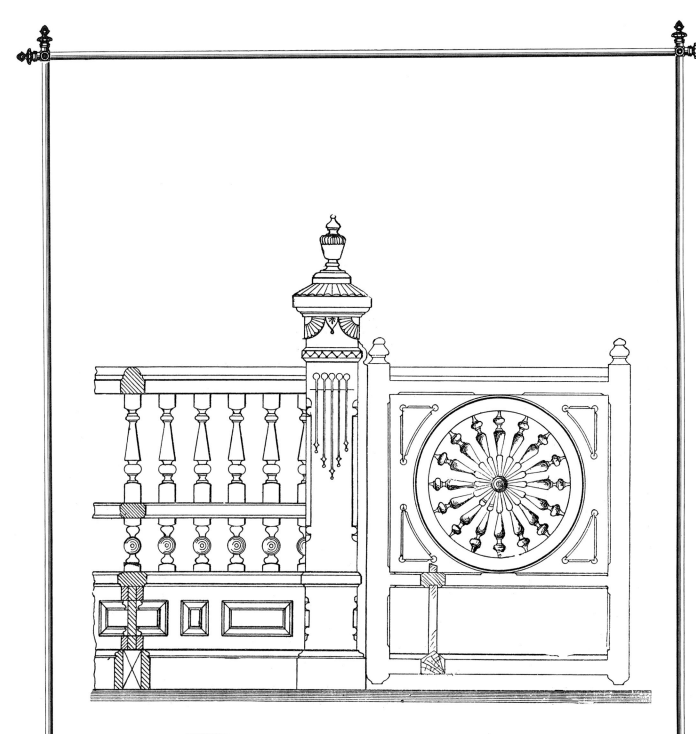

FENCE.   _GATE._

DESIGN No. 97.

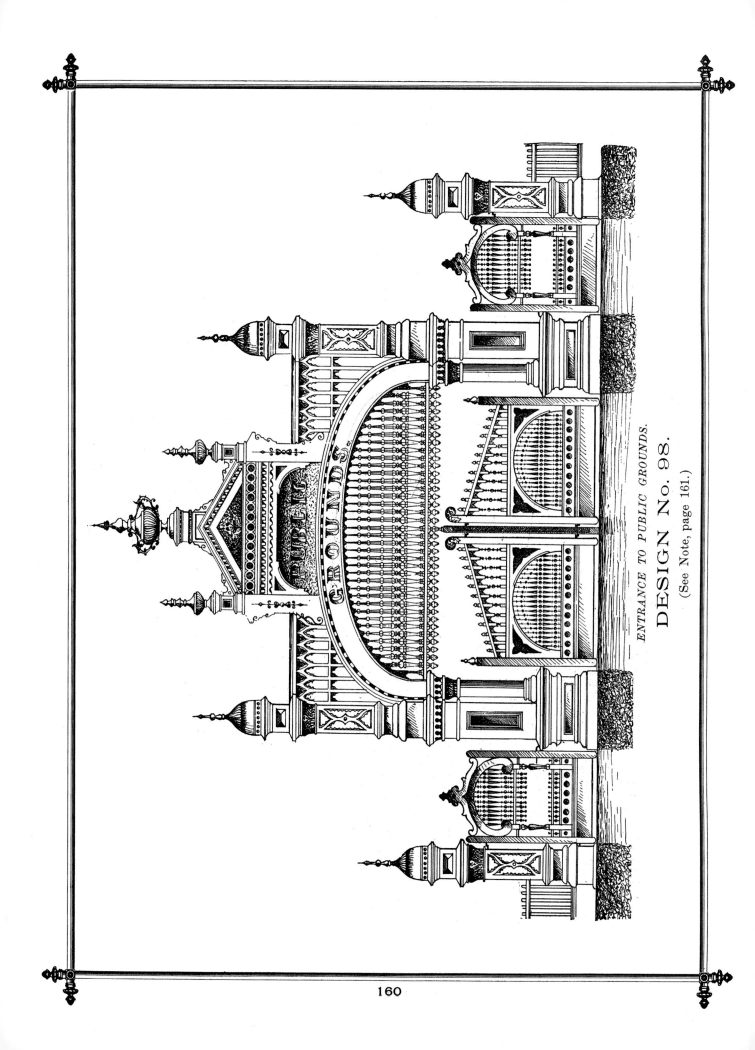

ENTRANCE TO PUBLIC GROUNDS.

DESIGN No. 98.

(See Note, page 161.)

PUBLIC GROUNDS

NOTE.

On this page is given a design for a double gate, together with a post and section of a fence, which can be used as an entrance to a small cemetery or other public grounds. The scale is ¾ inch to the foot.

On page 160 is a design for a rich and elaborate entrance, suitable for any public grounds, such as a cemetery, park, fair grounds, &c., &c. Height from the ground to the cross rail under main arch is 12 feet; width between posts, 20 feet. Cost to build, in wood, about $300 to $500; in stone and iron, from $1,500 to $2,500, and as high as $3,000.

This structure, painted in proper colors and tastefully gilded would produce a magnificent effect.

LARGE ENTRANCE GATE.

DESIGN No. 99.

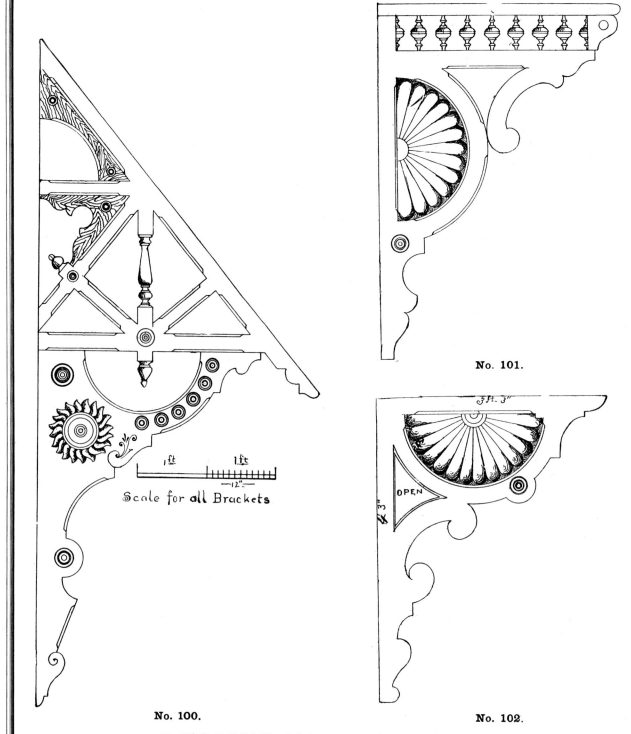

Scale for all Brackets

No. 101.

No. 100.

No. 102.

DESIGNS FOR BRACKETS.

NOTE.

On this and the following pages are given designs for brackets, mostly ornamental and all new and not to be found on any of the designs of cottages in this work. Plain ones are not given, as most any one can make such without any pattern. No prices are given. They can be applied to almost any place requiring such brackets, as any one of them can be reduced to fit a smaller place than they are made for. The scale for all is given with design No. 100.

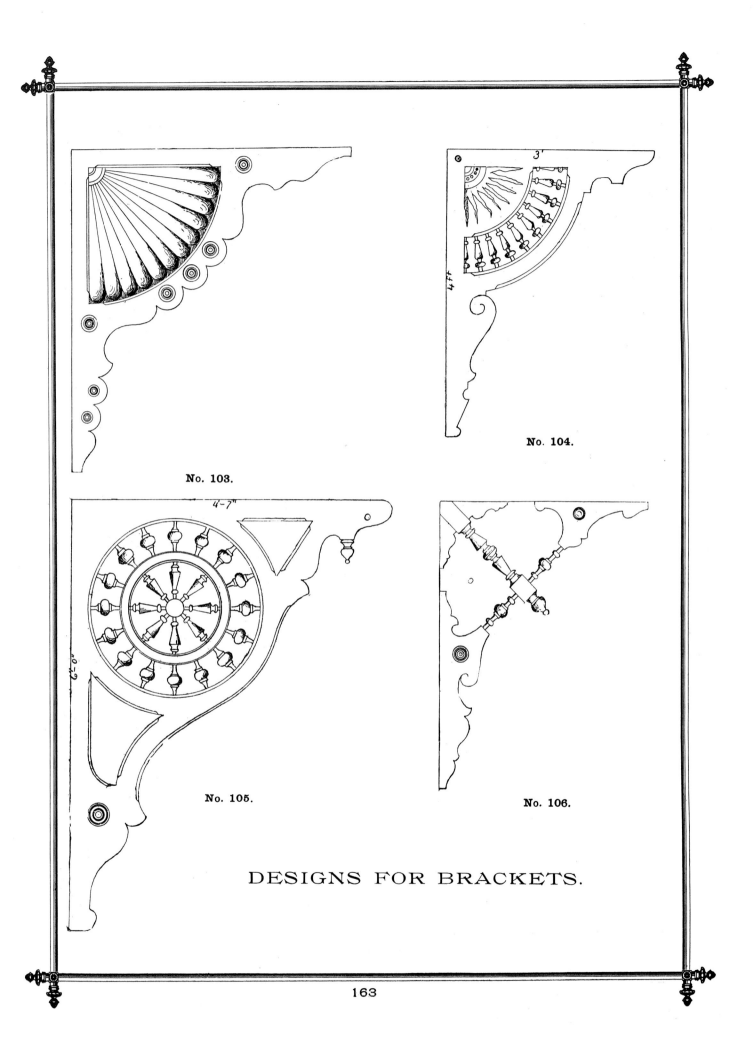

No. 103.

No. 104.

No. 105.

No. 106.

DESIGNS FOR BRACKETS.

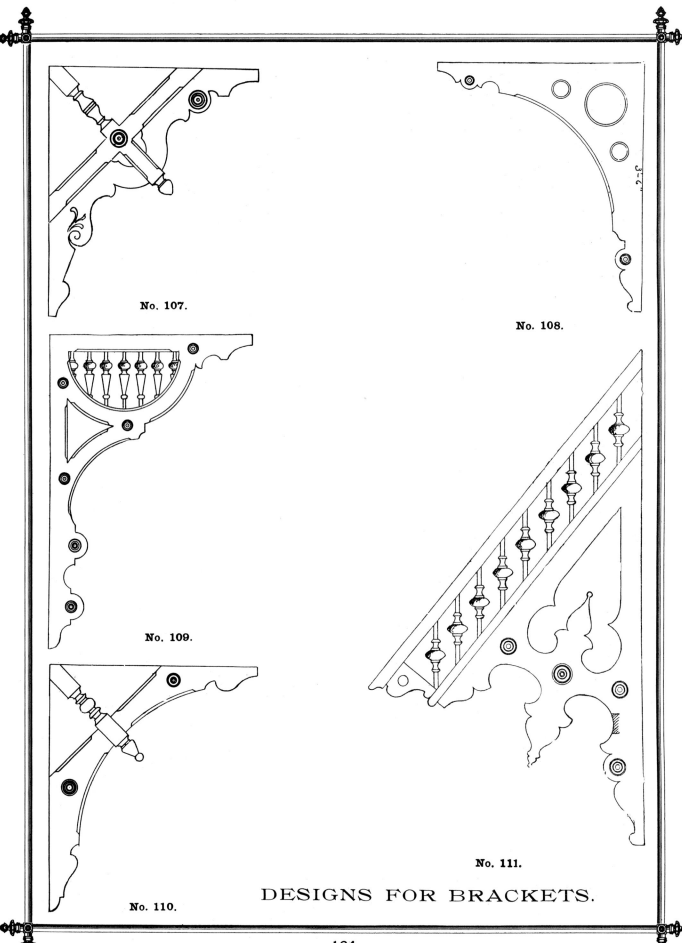

No. 107.

No. 108.

No. 109.

No. 111.

No. 110.

DESIGNS FOR BRACKETS.

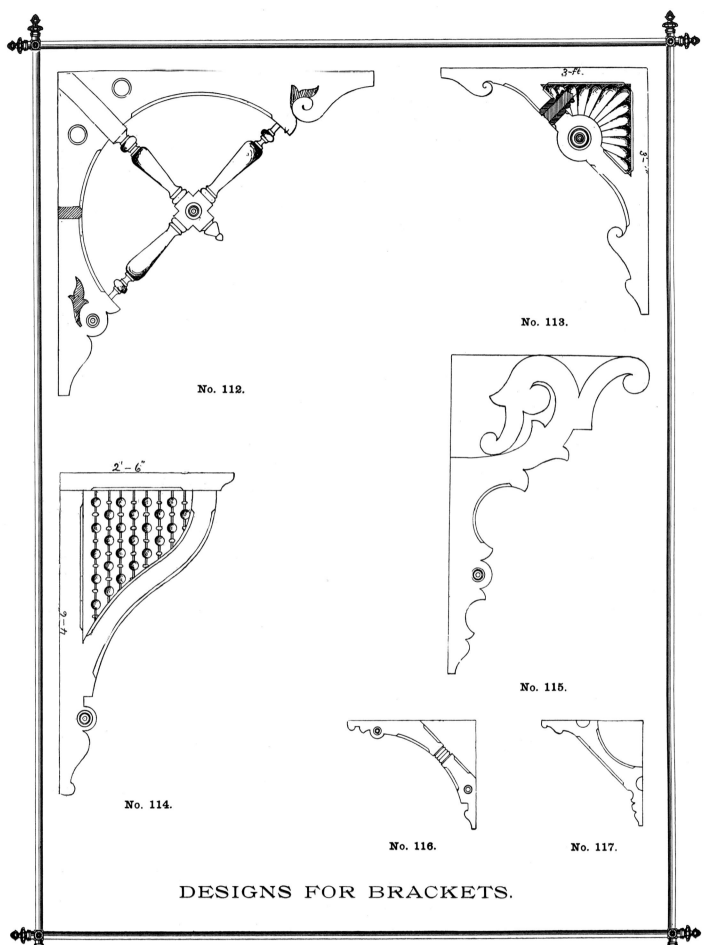

No. 113.

No. 112.

No. 115.

No. 114.

No. 116.

No. 117.

DESIGNS FOR BRACKETS.

REMARKS.

In this little cut we give the front elevation of the residence shown on page 118.

It is here presented in order to give one an idea of its proper proportions.

The hall staircase is shown on page 120.

The design works up handsomely.

REMARKS.

Below we give the floor plans of a residence similar to the design shown on page 14 and was erected by Mr. W. B. Earthman, at Murfreesboro, Tenn., at a cost of about $8,000. The arrangement of the rooms were worked up under the personal direction of Mrs. Earthman, and is considered a good example of a modern Southern residence. The rooms will be seen to be large and the stories are 11 feet and 10 feet high respectively.

FRONT VIEW OF DESIGN No. 55.

[See page 118.]

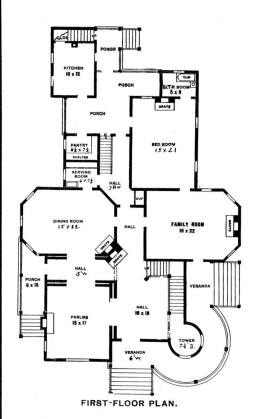

FIRST-FLOOR PLAN.

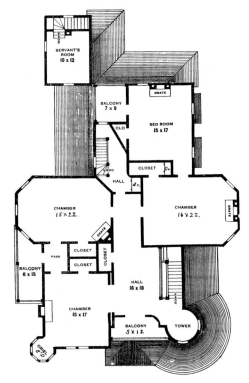

SECOND-FLOOR PLAN.

ENLARGED PLAN OF DESIGN No. 1, PAGE 14.

If you don't find your ideal plan in this book, write to us, suggesting changes you would like in the plan coming nearest your wants, or send us a rough sketch of the floor plans covering your ideas, giving near the amount you would like to spend in a house, and we will assist you in getting a handsome and convenient home. Don't be reluctant about writing to us.

PRICES

—OF—

Materials and Labor from which the Designs in this Book were Estimated.

Sheathing, per M...$15 00

Weatherboarding or Siding, per M 25 00

Flooring, per M.. 25 00

Outside Finish Lumber, per M... 38 00

Framing, per M.... .... 15 00

Shingles, per M... 4 50

Doors, No. 1, 2.8 x 8 x 1½, four panel, moulded two sides.... .... 2 50

Windows, glazed, 24 x 36, two lt., pine............................... 2 00

Window Blinds, outside... 1 50

Baseboards, per lineal foot 04

Head and Base Blocks, each... 10

Mouldings, per 1 in. section, 100 feet................................... 65

Pine Architraves, $\frac{7}{8}$ inch x 5 in., moulded........................ 03

Porch Columns, turned, 5 x 5, poplar................................... 1 75

Turned Balusters, 2 in. x 2 in. x 2 feet 6 in., each.... .... 12½

Turned Spindles, 6 in.. 06

Beaded Ceiling, per M... 25 00

Lath and Plaster, per square yard, three coats 28

Common Brick laid in wall, per M....................................... 15 00

Stone Wall, double faced, per cubic foot.......................... 25

Stone Wall, double faced, rubble, per perch....................... 4 25

Excavating, per cubic yard... 25

Painting, three coat work, per square yard 25

Slating, exclusive of all other roof materials, per square, 100 feet........ 8 00

Carpenters' work, per day... 2 50

Masons' work, per day ....$3 50 and 4 00

Hardwoods for interior finish, double that of pine or soft woods, as given above.

PRICES

—OF—

Plans, Specifications and Full Working Drawings for Designs shown in this Book.

[SEE PAGE 11.]

Design No.	Price.	Design No.	Price.
1	$45 00	46	$35 00
2	15 00	47	35 00
3	10 00	48	50 00
4	8 50	49	30 00
5	10 00	50	40 00
6	10 00	51	45 00
7	10 00	52	60 00
8	10 00	53	55 00
9	12 00	54	35 00
10	10 00	55	40 00
11	12 50	56	38 00
12	15 00	57	7 00
13	15 00	58	7 00
14	12 50	59	47 00
15	18 00	60	30 00
16	14 00	61	31 50
17	16 00	62	12 00
18	18 50	63	15 00
19	18 00	64	8 00
20	20 00	65	20 00
21	22 00	66	35 00
22	15 00	67	40 00
23	25 00	68	35 00
24	20 00	69	12 00
25	18 00	70, 75, 76 and 77, each	2 50
26	28 00	78	3 00
27	24 00	79	3 00
28	22 50	80	5 00
29	25 00	81	5 00
30	28 00	84	2 00
31	22 50	85	2 00
32	25 00	86	2 00
33	32 00	87	2 00
34	30 00	88	2 00
35	25 00	89	7 00
36	40 00	90	7 00
37	33 00	91	7 00
38	27 50	92	7 00
39	25 00	93	3 00
40	30 00	94	3 00
41	35 00	95	3 00
42	40 00	96	3 00
43 Plan No. 1, $25 00. No. 2,	18 00	97	3 00
44	40 00	98	20 00
45	38 00	99	3 00

Any of the above plans will be sent by express on receipt of the price, or will be sent C. O. D. if desired. Orders by mail or telegraph promptly attended to. Money may be sent by express, post-office order, registered letter or draft on New York. If sent in this way it is at our risk.

Address,

GEO. F. BARBER & CO., Knoxville, Tenn.

Graphic Worlds of Peter Bruegel the Elder, Peter Bruegel. 63 engravings and a woodcut made from the drawings of the 16th-century Flemish master: landscapes, seascapes, stately ships, drolleries, whimsical allegories, scenes from the Gospels, and much more. Stimulating commentaries by H. Arthur Klein on individual prints, bits of biography on etcher or engraver, and comparisons with Bruegel's original designs. 176pp. 9⅜ x 12¼. 21132-0

Views of Venice by Canaletto, Antonio Canaletto (engraved by Antonio Visentini). Unparalleled visual statement from early 18th century includes 14 scenes down the Grand Canal away from and returning to the Rialto Bridge, 12 magnificent views of the inimitable *campi,* and more. Extraordinarily handsome, large-format edition. Text by J. Links. 50 illustrations. 90pp. 13¾ x 10. 22705-7

The Craftsman's Handbook, Cennino Cennini. This fifteenth-century handbook reveals secrets and techniques of the masters in drawing, oil painting, frescoes, panel painting, gilding, casting, and more. 142pp. 6⅛ x 9¼. 20054-X

The Book of Kells, Blanche Cirker (ed.). Thirty-two full-color, full-page plates from the greatest illuminated manuscript of the Middle Ages; painstakingly reproduced from rare facsimile edition. Publisher's Note. Captions. 32pp. 9⅜ x 12¼. 24345-1

The Complete Engravings, Etchings and Drypoints of Albrecht Dürer, Albrecht Dürer. This splendid collection reproduces all 105 of Dürer's works in these media, including such well-known masterpieces as *Knight, Death and Devil, Melencolia I,* and *Adam and Eve,* plus portraits of such contemporaries as Erasmus and Frederick the Wise; popular and religious works; peasant scenes, and the portentous works: *The Four Witches, Sol Justitiae,* and *The Monstrous Sow of Landser.* 120 plates. 235pp. 8⅜ x 11¼. 22851-7

The Human Figure, Albrecht Dürer. This incredible collection contains drawings in which Dürer experimented with many methods: the "anthropometric system," learned from Leonardo; the "exempeda" method, known to most as the man inscribed in a circle; the human figure in motion; and much more. Some of the life studies rank among the finest ever done. 170 plates. 355pp. 8⅜ x 11¼. 21042-1

Medieval Woodcut Illustrations, Carol Belanger Grafton (ed.). Selections from a 1493 history of the world features magnificent woodcuts of 91 locales, plus 143 illustrations of figures and decorative objects. Comparable to the Gutenberg Bible in terms of craftsmanship; designed by Pleydenwuff and Wolgemut. Permission-free. 194 b/w illustrations. 80pp. 8⅜ x 11. 40458-7

Engravings of Hogarth, William Hogarth. Collection of 101 robust engravings reveals the life of the drawing rooms, inns, and alleyways of 18th-century England through the eyes of a great satirist. Includes all the major series: *Rake's Progress, Harlot's Progress,* Illustrations for *Hudibras, Before and After, Beer Street,* and *Gin Lane,* plus 96 more with commentary by Sean Shesgreen. xxxiii+205pp. 11 x 13¾. 22479-1

The Dance of Death, Hans Holbein the Younger. Most celebrated of Holbein's works. Unabridged reprint of the original 1538 masterpiece and one of the great graphic works of the era. Forty-one striking woodcuts capture the motif *Memento mori*–"Remember, you will die." Includes translations of all quotes and verses. 146pp. 5⅜ x 8½. 22804-5

The Complete Woodcuts of Albrecht Dürer, Dr. W. Kurth (ed.). Superb collection of 346 extant woodcuts: the celebrated series on the *Life of Virgin, the Apocalypse of St. John, the Great Passion, St. Jerome in His Study, Samson Fighting the Lion, The Fall of Icarus, The Rhinoceros, the Triumphal Arch, Saints and Biblical Scenes,* and many others, including much little-known material. 285pp. 8½ x 12¼. 21097-9

Religious Art in France of the Thirteenth Century, Emile Mâle. This classic by a noted art historian focuses on French cathedrals of the 13th century as the apotheosis of the medieval style. Topics include iconography, bestiaries, illustrated calendars, the gospels, secular history, and many other aspects. 190 b/w illustrations. 442pp. 5⅜ x 8½. 41061-7

Great Scenes from the Bible: 230 Magnificent 17th Century Engravings, Matthaeus Merian (the Elder). Remarkably detailed illustrations depict Adam and Eve Driven Out of the Garden of Eden, The Flood, David Slaying Goliath, Christ in the Manger, The Raising of Lazarus, The Crucifixion, and many other scenes. A wonderful pictorial dimension to age-old stories. All plates from the classic 1625 edition. 128pp. 9 x 12. 42043-4

Medieval and Renaissance Treatises on the Arts of Painting: Original Texts with English Translations, Mary P. Merrifield. This rare 1849 work reprints treatises from the 12th–17th centuries (with the original-language version and its English translation on facing pages). Oil painting practices, methods of mixing pigments, and much more, with commentary on each treatise, plus excellent introduction discussing social history, artistic practices. 1,280pp. 5⅜ x 8½. 40440-4

Views of Rome Then and Now, Giovanni Battista Piranesi and Herschel Levit. Piranesi's masterful representations of architecture are reprinted in large format alongside corresponding recent photos. Monuments of ancient, early Christian, Renaissance, and Baroque Rome (Colosseum, Forum, fountains, etc.) with auxiliary notes on both the etchings and photos. 82 plates. 109pp. 11 x 14¾. 23339-1

The Notebooks of Leonardo Da Vinci, compiled and edited by Jean Paul Richter. These 1,566 extracts reveal the full range of Leonardo's versatile genius: his writings on painting, sculpture, architecture, anatomy, mining, inventions, and music. The first volume is devoted to various aspects of art: structure of the eye and vision, perspective, science of light and shade, color theory, and more. The second volume shows the wide range of Leonardo's secondary interests: geography, warfare, zoology, medicine, astronomy, and other topics. Dual Italian-English texts, with 186 plates and more than 500 additional drawings faithfully reproduced. Total of 913pp. 7⅞ x 10¾. Vol. I: 22572-0 Vol. II: 22573-9

On Divers Arts, Theophilus (translated by John G. Hawthorne and C. S. Smith). Twelfth-century treatise on arts written by a practicing artist. Pigments, glass blowing, stained glass, gold and silver work, and more. Authoritative edition of a medieval classic. 34 illustrations. 216pp. 6½ x 9¼. 23784-2

The Complete Etchings of Rembrandt: Reproduced in Original Size, Rembrandt van Rijn. One of the greatest figures in Western Art, Rembrandt van Rijn (1606–1669) brought etching to a state of unsurpassed perfection. This edition includes more than 300 works–portraits, landscapes, biblical scenes, allegorical and mythological pictures, and more–reproduced in full size directly from a rare collection of etchings famed for its pristine condition, rich contrasts, and brilliant printing. With detailed captions, chronology of Rembrandt's life and etchings, discussion of the technique of etching in this time, and a bibliography. 224pp. 9⅜ x 12¼. 28181-7

Drawings of Rembrandt, Seymour Slive (ed.) Updated Lippmann, Hofstede de Groot edition, with definitive scholarly apparatus. Many drawings are preliminary sketches for great paintings and sketchings. Others are self-portraits, beggars, children at play, biblical sketches, landscapes, nudes, Oriental figures, birds, domestic animals, episodes from mythology, classical studies, and more. Also, a selection of work by pupils and followers. Total of 630pp. 9⅛ x 12¼. Vol. I 21485-0 Vol. II 21486-9

The Materials and Techniques of Medieval Painting, Daniel V. Thompson. Sums up 20th-century knowledge: paints, binders, metals, and surface preparation. 239pp. 5⅜ x 8½. 20327-1

Drawings of Albrecht Dürer, Heinrich Wölfflin (ed.). 81 plates show development from youth to full style: *Dürer's Wife Agnes, Idealistic Male and Female Figures* (Adam and Eve), *The Lamentation,* and many others. The editor not only introduces the drawings with an erudite essay, but also supplies captions for each, telling about the circumstances of the work, its relation to other works, and significant features. 173pp. 8⅛ x 11. 22352-3

*Write for **free** Fine Art and Art Instruction Catalog to*
Dover Publications, Inc., Dept. ABI, 31 East 2nd Street, Mineola, NY 11501
*Visit us online at **www.doverpublications.com***

Nineteenth-Century Art

Great Drawings and Illustrations from Punch, 1841–1901, Stanley Appelbaum and Richard Kelly (eds.). Golden years of British illustration. 192 drawings by 25 artists: Phiz, Leech, Tenniel, du Maurier, Sambourne. 144pp. 9 x 12. 24110-6

Best Works of Aubrey Beardsley, Aubrey Beardsley. Rich selection of 170 boldly executed black-and-white illustrations ranging from illustrations for Laclos' *Les Liaisons Dangereuses* and Balzac's *La Comédie Humaine* to magazine cover designs, book plates, title-page ornaments for books, silhouettes, and delightful mini-portraits of major composers. 160pp. 8⅛ x 11. 26273-1

The Rape of the Lock, Aubrey Beardsley and Alexander Pope. Reproduction of "ideal" 1896 edition in which text, typography, and illustration complement each other. 10 great illustrations capture the mock-heroic, delicate fancy of Pope's poem. 47pp. 8⅛ x 11. 21963-1

Salome, Aubrey Beardsley and Oscar Wilde. Lord Alfred Douglas' translation of Wilde's great play (originally written in French,) with all 20 well-known Beardsley illustrations including suppressed plates. Introduction by Robert Ross. xxii+69pp. 8⅛ x 11. 21830-9

Drawings of William Blake, William Blake. Fine reproductions show the range of Blake's artistic genius: drawings for *The Book of Job, The Divine Comedy, Paradise Lost,* an edition of Shakespeare's plays, grotesques and visionary heads, mythological figures, and other drawings. Selection, introduction, and commentary by Sir Geoffrey Keynes. 178pp. 8⅛ x 11. 22303-5

Songs of Innocence, William Blake. The first and most popular of Blake's famous "Illuminated Books" in a facsimile edition. 31 illustrations, text of each poem. 64pp. 5¼ x 7. 22764-2

A Cézanne Sketchbook: Figures, Portraits, Landscapes and Still Lifes, Paul Cézanne. Experiments with tonal effects, light, mass, and other qualities in more than 100 drawings. A revealing view of developing master painter, precursor of cubism. 102 illustrations. 144pp. 8⅜ x 6⅜. 24790-2

Graphic Works of George Cruikshank, George Cruikshank (Richard A. Vogler, ed.). 269 permission-free illustrations (8 in full color) reproduced directly from original etchings and woodcuts. Introduction, notes. 200pp. 9⅜ x 12¼. 23438-X

Daumier: 10 Great Lithographs, Honoré Daumier. Works range from early and caustic anti-government drawings in 1831 to last works prior to retirement in 1872. Collection concentrates on liberated women, the French bourgeoisie, actors, musicians, soldiers, teachers, lawyers, married life, and myriad other creations by the "Michelangelo of the people." 158pp. 9⅜ x 12¼. 23512-2

Degas' Drawings, H. G. E. Degas. Dancers, nudes, portraits, travel scenes, and other works in inimitable style, most not available anywhere else. 100 plates, 8 in color. 100pp. 9 x 12. 21233-5

The Doré Bible Illustrations, Gustave Doré. 241 detailed plates from the Bible: the Creation scenes, Adam and Eve, horrifying visions of the Flood, the battle sequences with their monumental crowds, depictions of the life of Jesus, and visions of the new Jerusalem. Each plate is accompanied by the appropriate verses from the King James version. 241pp. 9 x 12. 23004-X

The Doré Gallery: His 120 Greatest Illustrations, Gustave Doré (Carol Belanger Grafton, ed.). Comprising the finest plates from the great illustrator's work, this collection features outstanding engravings from such literary classics as Milton's *Paradise Lost, The Divine Comedy* by Dante, Coleridge's *The Rime of the Ancient Mariner, The Raven* by Poe, Sue's *The Wandering Jew,* and many others. Captions. 128pp. 9 x 12. 40160-X

Doré's Illustrations of the Crusades, Gustave Doré. Magnificent compilation of all 100 original plates from Ichaud's classic *History of the Crusades.* Includes *The War Cry of the Crusaders, The Massacre of Antioch, The Road to Jerusalem, the Baptism of Infidels, the Battle of Lepanto,* and many more. Captions. 112pp. 9 x 12. 29597-4

Doré's Illustrations for Don Quixote, Gustave Doré. Here are 190 wood-engraved plates, 120 full-page: charging the windmill, traversing Spanish plains, valleys, and mountains; ghostly visions of dragons, knights, and flaming lake. Marvelous detail, minutiae, accurate costumes, architecture, enchantment, pathos, and humor. Captions. 160pp. 9 x 12. 24300-1

The Rime of the Ancient Mariner, Gustave Doré and Samuel Taylor Coleridge. Doré's dramatic engravings for *The Rime of the Ancient Mariner* are considered by many to be his greatest work. The terrifying space of the open sea, the storms and whirlpools of an unknown ocean, the ice of the Antarctica, and more–all are rendered in a powerful manner. Full text. 38 plates. 77pp. 9¼ x 12. 22305-1

Gauguin's Intimate Journals, Paul Gauguin. Revealing documents, reprinted from rare, limited edition, throw much light on the painter's inner life, his tumultuous relationship with van Gogh, evaluations of Degas, Monet, and other artists; hatred of hypocrisy and sham, life in the Marquesas Islands, and much more. 27 full-page illustrations by Gauguin. Preface by Emil Gauguin. 160pp. 6½ x 9¼. 29441-2

Noa Noa: The Tahitian Journal, Paul Gauguin. Celebrated journal records the artist's thoughts and impressions during two years he spent in Tahiti. Compelling autobiographical fragment. 24 b/w illustrations. 96pp. 5⅜ x 8½. 24859-3

Los Caprichos, Francisco Goya. Considered Goya's most brilliant work, this collection combines corrosive satire and exquisite technique to depict 18th-century Spain as a nation of grotesque monsters sprung up in the absence of reason. Captions. 183pp. 6⅜ x 9⅜. 22384-1

Ornamentation and Illustrations from the Kelmscott Chaucer, William Morris. Beautiful permission-free tailpieces, decorative letters, elaborate floral borders and frames, samples of body type, and all 98 delicate woodcut illustrations. xiv+112pp. 8½ x 12. 22970-X

William Morris on Art and Socialism, William Morris (Norman Kelvin, ed.). This outstanding collection of 11 lectures and an essay, delivered between 1881 and 1896, illustrates Morris' conviction that the primary human pleasure lies in making and using items of utility and beauty. Selections include: "Art: A Serious Thing," "Art Under Plutocracy," "Useful Work vs. Useless Toil," "The Dawn of a New Epoch," "Of the Origins of Ornamental Art," "The Society of the Future," and "The Present Outlook of Socialism." Introduction. Biographical Note. 208pp. 5⅜ x 8½. 40904-X

The Life of William Morris, J.W. Mackail. Classic biography of great Victorian poet, designer, and socialist. Childhood, education, embrace of socialism, Arts & Crafts movement, Kelmscott Press, and much more. 22 illustrations. 800pp. 5⅜ x 8½. 28793-9

Degas, Julius Meier-Graefe. Famous art critic's lively, intimate, highly perceptive study of the artist's life and work. Many valuable insights and fascinating anecdotes. 40 finely reproduced black-and-white plates. 128pp. 5⅜ x 8½. 25702-9

Great Ballet Prints of the Romantic Era, Parmenia Migel. Sumptuous collection from 1830 to 1860. Taglioni, Elssler, Grisi, and other stars by such artists as Chalon, Grevedon, Deveria, etc. Introduction. 128pp. 9 x 12. 24050-9

Great Lithographs by Toulouse-Lautrec: 89 Plates, H. Toulouse-Lautrec. Exceptional sampling of some of finest lithographs ever. 89 plates, including 8 in full color. 88pp. 9⅜ x 12¼. 24359-1

Cézanne, Ambroise Vollard. French art dealer's intriguing memoirs of Cézanne–his life in Paris and Aix, friendship with Zola, passions, eccentricities. 20 paintings. 160pp. 5⅜ x 8½. 24729-5

Degas: An Intimate Portrait, Ambroise Vollard. Charming, anecdotal memoir by famous art dealer of one of the greatest 19th-century French painters. 14 illustrations. Introduction by Harold L. Van Doren. 96pp. 5⅜ x 8½. 25702-9

Renoir: An Intimate Record, Ambroise Vollard. Art dealer and publisher Vollard's splendid portrait of Renoir emerges in a long series of informal conversations with the Impressionist master that reveal intimate details of his life and career. 19 black-and-white illustrations of Renoir's paintings. 160pp. 5⅜ x 8½. 26488-2

The Life and Works of Augustus Saint Gaudens, Burke Wilkinson. Critically acclaimed work, nominated for Pulitzer Prize in 1986, vividly evokes life and work of great American sculptor. 64 b/w photos. Notes. Index. 480pp. 6 x 9. (Not available in United Kingdom). 27149-8

*Write for **free** Fine Art and Art Instruction Catalog to*
Dover Publications, Inc., Dept. ABI, 31 East 2nd Street, Mineola, NY 11501
*Visit us online at **www.doverpublications.com***

VICTORIAN HOUSEWARE, HARDWARE AND KITCHENWARE: A PICTORIAL ARCHIVE WITH OVER 2000 ILLUSTRATIONS, Ronald S. Barlow (ed.). This fascinating archive, reprinted from rare woodcut engravings and selected from hard-to-find antique trade catalogs, offers a realistic view of the furnishings of a typical 19th-century home, including andirons, ash sifters, housemaids' buckets, buttonhole cutters, sausage stuffers, seed strippers, spittoons, and hundreds of other items. Captions include size, weight, and cost. 376pp. 9⅜ x 12¼. 41727-1

BEARDSLEY'S LE MORTE DARTHUR: SELECTED ILLUSTRATIONS, Aubrey Beardsley. His illustrations for the great Thomas Malory classic made Aubrey Beardsley famous virtually overnight–and fired the imaginations of generations of artists with what became known as the "Beardsley look." This volume contains a rich selection of those splendid drawings, including floral and foliated openings, fauns and satyrs, initials, ornaments, and much more. Characters from Arthurian legend are portrayed in splendid full-page illustrations, bordered with evocative and fecund sinuosities of plant and flower. Artists and designers will find here a source of superb designs, graphics, and motifs for permission-free use. 62 black-and-white illustrations. 48pp. 8¼ x 11. 41795-6

TREASURY OF BIBLE ILLUSTRATIONS: OLD AND NEW TESTAMENTS, Julius Schnorr von Carolsfeld. All the best-loved, most-quoted Bible stories, painstakingly reproduced from a rare volume of German engravings. 179 imaginative illustrations depict 105 episodes from Old Testament, 74 scenes from New Testament–each on a separate page, with chapter, verse, King James Text. Outstanding source of permission-free art; remarkably accessible treatment of the Scriptures. x+182pp. 8⅜ x 11¼. 40703-9

3200 OLD-TIME CUTS AND ORNAMENTS, Blanche Cirker (ed.). Permission-free pictures from 1909 French typography catalog: plants, animals, religious motifs, music, carriages, boats, sports, furniture, clothing; plus borders, banners, wreaths, and other ornaments. More than 3,200 b/w illustrations. 112pp. 9⅜ x 12¼. 41732-8

A DIDEROT PICTORIAL ENCYCLOPEDIA OF TRADES AND INDUSTRY, Denis Diderot. First paperbound edition of 485 remarkable plates from the great 18th-century reference work. Permission-free plates depict vast array of arts and trades before the Industrial Revolution. Two-volume set. Total of 936pp. 9 x 12.

    Vol. I: Agriculture and rural arts, fishing, art of war, metalworking, mining. Plates 1–208. 27428-4
    Vol. II: Glass, masonry, carpentry, textiles, printing, leather, gold and jewelry, fashion, miscellaneous trades. Plates 209–485. Indexes of persons, places, and subjects. 27429-2

BIRDS, FLOWERS AND BUTTERFLIES STAINED GLASS PATTERN BOOK, Connie Clough Eaton. 68 exquisite full-page patterns; lush baskets, vases, garden bouquets, birds, and more. Perfectly rendered for stained glass; suitable for many other arts and crafts projects. 12 color illustrations on covers. 64pp. 8¼ x 11. 40717-9

TURN-OF-THE-CENTURY TILE DESIGNS IN FULL COLOR, L. François. 250 designs brimming with Art Nouveau flavor: beautiful floral and foliate motifs on wall tiles for bathrooms, multicolored stenciled friezes, and more. 48pp. 9¼ x 12¼. 41525-2

CHILDREN: A PICTORIAL ARCHIVE OF PERMISSION-FREE ILLUSTRATIONS, Carol Belanger Grafton (ed.). More than 850 versatile illustrations from rare sources depict engaging moppets playing with toys, dolls, and pets; riding bicycles; playing tennis and baseball; reading, sleeping; engaged in activities with other children; and in many other settings and situations. Appealing vignettes of bygone times for artists, designers, and craftworkers. 96pp. 9 x 12. 41797-2

504 DECORATIVE VIGNETTES IN FULL COLOR, Carol Belanger Grafton (ed.). Permission-free Victorian images of animals (some dressed in quaint period costumes, others fancifully displaying brief messages), angels, fans, cooks, clowns, musicians, revelers, and many others. 40467-6

OLD-TIME CHRISTMAS VIGNETTES IN FULL COLOR, Carol Belanger Grafton (ed.). 363 permission-free illustrations from vintage publications include Father Christmas, evergreen garlands, heavenly creatures, a splendidly decorated old-fashioned Christmas tree, and Victorian youngsters playing with Christmas toys, holding bouquets of holly, and much more. 40255-X

OLD-TIME NAUTICAL AND SEASHORE VIGNETTES IN FULL COLOR, Carol Belanger Grafton (ed.). More than 300 exquisite illustrations of sailors, ships, rowboats, lighthouses, swimmers, fish, shells, and other nautical motifs in a great variety of sizes, shapes, and styles–lovingly culled from rare 19th- and early-20th-century chromolithographs. 41524-4

BIG BOOK OF ANIMAL ILLUSTRATIONS, Maggie Kate (ed.). 688 up-to-date, detailed line illustrations–all permission-free–of monkeys and apes, horses, snakes, reptiles and amphibians, insects, butterflies, dinosaurs, and more, in accurate, natural poses. Index. 128pp. 9 x 12. 40464-1

422 ART NOUVEAU DESIGNS AND MOTIFS IN FULL COLOR, J. Klinger and H. Anker. Striking reproductions from a rare French portfolio of plants, animals, birds, insects, florals, abstracts, women, landscapes, and other subjects. Permission-free borders, repeating patterns, mortised cuts, corners, frames, and other configurations–all depicted in the sensuous, curvilinear Art Nouveau style. 32pp. 9¼ x 12¼. 40705-5

ANIMAL STUDIES: 550 ILLUSTRATIONS OF MAMMALS, BIRDS, FISH AND INSECTS, M. Méheut. Painstakingly reproduced from a rare original edition, this lavish bestiary features a spectacular array of creatures from the animal kingdom–mammals, fish, birds, reptiles and amphibians, and insects. Permission-free illustrations for graphics projects; marvelous browsing for antiquarians, art enthusiasts, and animal lovers. Captions. 112pp. 9⅜ x 12¼. 40266-5

THE ART NOUVEAU STYLE BOOK OF ALPHONSE MUCHA, Alphonse Mucha. Fine permission-free reproductions of all plates in Mucha's innovative portfolio, including designs for jewelry, wallpaper, stained glass, furniture, and tableware, plus figure studies, plant and animal motifs, and more. 18 plates in full color, 54 in 2 or more colors. Only complete one-volume edition. 80pp. 9⅜ x 12¼. 24044-4

ELEGANT FLORAL DESIGNS FOR ARTISTS AND CRAFTSPEOPLE, Marty Noble. More than 150 exquisite designs depict borders of fanciful flowers; filigreed compositions of floral sprays, wreaths, and single blossoms; delicate butterflies with wings displaying a patchwork mosaic; nosegays wrapped in lacy horns; and much more. A graceful, permission-free garden of flowers for use by illustrators, commercial artists, designers, and craftworkers. 64pp. 8¼ x 11. 42177-5

SNOWFLAKE DESIGNS, Marty Noble and Eric Gottesman. More than 120 intricate, permission-free images of snowflakes, based on actual photographs, are ideal for use in textile and wallpaper designs, needlework and craft projects, and other creative applications. iv+44pp. 8¼ x 11. 41526-0

ART NOUVEAU FIGURATIVE DESIGNS, Ed Sibbett, Jr. Art Nouveau goddesses, nymphs, florals from posters, decorations by Alphonse Mucha. 3 gorgeous designs. 48pp. 8¼ x 11. 23444-4

ANTIQUE FURNITURE AND DECORATIVE ACCESSORIES: A PICTORIAL ARCHIVE WITH 3,500 ILLUSTRATIONS, Thomas Arthur Strange. Cathedral stalls, altar pieces, sofas, commodes, writing tables, grillwork, organs, pulpits, and other decorative accessories produced by such noted craftsmen as Inigo Jones, Christopher Wren, Sheraton, Hepplewhite, and Chippendale. Descriptive text. 376pp. 8⅜ x 11¼. 41224-5

ART NOUVEAU FLORAL PATTERNS AND STENCIL DESIGNS IN FULL COLOR, M. P. Verneuil. Permission-free art from two rare turn-of-the-century portfolios (*Etude de la Plante* and *L'ornementation par le Pochoir*) includes 159 floral and foliate motifs by M. P. Verneuil, one of the Art Nouveau movement's finest artists. The collection includes 120 images of flowers–foxglove, hollyhocks, columbine, lilies, and others–and 39 stencil designs of blossoming trees, reeds, mushrooms, oak leaves, peacocks, and more. 80pp. 9¼ x 12¼. 40126-X